THE ISLE OF MULL

About the Author

Terry Marsh is a full-time, award-winning outdoor and travel writer and photographer who has authored, co-authored or revised more than 90 travel or walking guidebooks. He first visited Mull more than 20 years ago, and has been returning ever since. He is Fellow of the Royal Geographical Society and of the Society of Antiquaries of Scotland, and holds a Master of Arts degree from Lancaster University.

Other Cicerone guides by the author

Great Mountain Days in
   Snowdonia
The Isle of Skye
The West Highland Way
A Northern Coast-to-Coast Walk
The Dales Way

The Shropshire Way (with Julie
   Meech)
Walking on the Isle of Man
Walking in the Forest of Bowland
   and Pendle
Walking on the West Pennine
   Moors

THE ISLE OF MULL

by
Terry Marsh

2 POLICE SQUARE, MILNTHORPE, CUMBRIA LA7 7PY
www.cicerone.co.uk

Printed by MCC Graphics, Spain

A catalogue record for this book is available from the British Library.
All photographs are by the author unless otherwise stated.

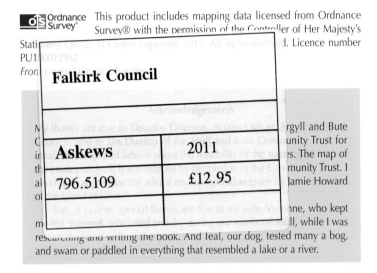
Falkirk Council

Askews	2011
796.5109	£12.95

Acknowledgements

My thanks are due to Douglas Grierson, Access Officer ... rgyll and Bute C... and to Ian Dunlop of the Mull and Iona Community Trust for in... ... advice about the feasibility of the routes. The map of th... ... is reproduced by ... ion of the Community Trust. I al... ... the advice and ... ion given ... Jamie Howard of ... ... of Libraries

But, of course, special thanks are due to my wife, Vivienne, who kept me fed, watered, motivated ... ... on Mull, while I was researching and writing the book. And Teal, our dog, tested many a bog, and swam or paddled in everything that resembled a lake or a river.

Advice to Readers

Readers are advised that, while every effort is made by our authors to ensure the accuracy of guidebooks as they go to print, changes can occur during the lifetime of an edition. Please check Updates on this book's page on the Cicerone website (www.cicerone.co.uk) before planning your trip. We would also advise that you check information about such things as transport, accommodation and shops locally. Even rights of way can be altered over time. We are always grateful for information about any discrepancies between a guide and the facts on the ground, sent by email to info@cicerone.co.uk or by post to Cicerone, 2 Police Square, Milnthorpe LA7 7PY, United Kingdom.

CONTENTS

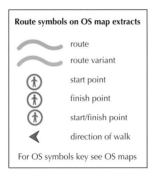

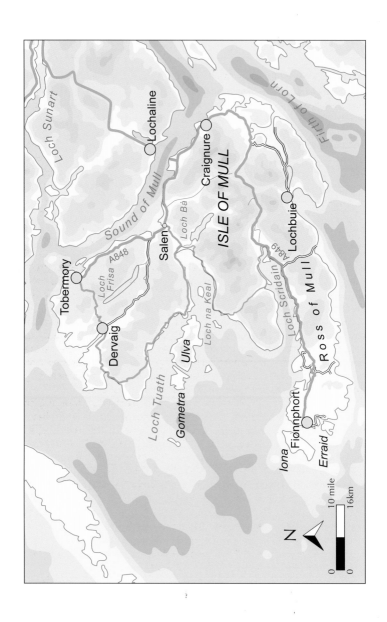

Loch Sunart

Loch Sunart

Lochaline

Craignure

ISLE OF MULL

Firth of Lorn

Sound of Mull

Loch Bà

Salen

Lochbuie

A848

Tobermory

Loch Frisa

A849

Loch na Keal

Dervaig

Loch Scridain

Ross of Mull

Loch Tuath

Ulva

Gometra

Iona

Fionnphort

Erraid

10 mile

16km

N

0

0

PREFACE

I don't know when I first visited Mull; certainly it was more than 20, or even 25, years ago. I have been visiting the Inner Hebrides, notably Skye, for over 40 years. For sure, it was during the courtship years of my love affair with Scottish islands, a time when I was receptive to a whole litany of moods, impressions, atmospheric nuances (that is, abrupt and unpleasant weather changes), cultural differences and the sort of free-range possibilities that later led to a book about all the Scottish islands. One thing is certain, it was the superb writing of Jim Crumley, first about Skye and then in *The Heart of Mull*, that was a catalyst, completely changing the way I saw and understood what I was looking at. I met Jim once, on Beinn Ime above Loch Lomond – he was coming down as I was going up. We chatted briefly, and it turned out we had friends in common. Little did I know then how much his writing would influence my own way of thinking.

So, after three editions of my guide to walking on Skye, it was time to turn my attention to Mull and its islands. And what a joy it has been. Like Skye, Mull has the full range of walking country. There is clearly less of the craggy stuff that you get in the Cuillin but anyone who loves walking on islands, where the sea is always somewhere in view, will enjoy what Mull has to offer, and be surprised by the diversity and richness of this magnificent landscape.

For the walker, whatever his or her fitness, Mull is a great walking destination, offering easy routes to draw you in and then, on longer but no less enjoyable walks, putting you in your place as you struggle with some of its difficulties. Here you can enjoy long and lonely days among the hills or wandering the coastline, often on splendid raised beaches. Or simply potter along shorter walks, or amble through forests, enjoying the natural history for which Mull is renowned.

This book was written while staying at a former shepherd's cottage in Glen Forsa, with Highland cattle frequently grazing at the gate or scratching their heads on the gate posts, red deer passing by the door, hen harriers out for lunch, and, far from city lights, night-time views of the Milky Way as clear as could be. Yesterday the light up the glen was amazing, and the walk to its head below Beinn Talaidh quite superb. Today it's all I can do to see the chaffinches feeding on the nuts on the garden. These extremes are what I find so fascinating about Mull. You get them almost anywhere in Britain, but there is something soothing about Mull, something that makes you want to be out, in the heart of Mull, getting beneath its skin…it's not unusual to see people of all ages standing by the roadside just look-ing, mesmerised, as if they have never seen a landscape quite this one.

But so changeable is Mull that you can never experience it all in one visit; you will simply have to come back, often and again.

Terry Marsh

Glen Aros and distant view of Loch Frisa (Walk 1.16)

INTRODUCTION

An t-Eilean Muileach, an t-eilean aghmhor,
An t-Eilean grianach mu'n iath an saile,
Eilean buadhmhor nam fuar bheann arda,
Nan coilltean uaine, 's cluaintean fasail.

The Isle of Mull, of Isles the fairest,
Of ocean's gems 'tis the first and rarest;
Green grassy island of sparkling fountains,
Of dark green woods and tow'ring mountains.
Dugald MacPhail (An t'Eilean Muileach)

With a diversity of land forms une-qualled by any other Scottish island, Mull is a place of wild beauty: untamed, rugged and never unin-teresting. Great swathes of Mull are approachable only on foot, and while there are roads (240km/150 miles of them), the abiding impression is that they are incidental, in a very minor way, to life on the island.

Separated from the Scottish mainland by the Sound of Mull and the Firth of Lorn, Mull, with an area of just under 90,000 hectares, is the

Calgary Bay (Walk 1.9)

11

fourth largest of the Hebridean islands (unless you want to play the pedant and claim that the larger Skye is no longer an island because someone built a bridge linking it with the mainland). With a coastline deeply penetrated by a ragged 480km (300 miles) of sea lochs and inlets that reward the visitor with constantly changing views, Mull is an island of delight and considerable variety. Indeed, it is the coastline that vies with the mountain heartlands as the island's most outstanding feature, offering towering cliffs and sandy bays, basalt columns and pink granite crags.

Geologically, Mull's origins are violently volcanic, but dramatised in such a complex evolution that the island is the stuff of dreams for geologists. The visiting walker soon comes to realise that it is this underlying foundation, the bones of the island, that provides a landscape both varied and demanding, blessed with considerable beauty and diversity. High (and not-so-high) mountains, remote glens, coastal paths along raised beaches, forest walks and island treks make Mull one of the most resourcefull of the Scottish islands for the walker. Although a great deal of the coastline is rugged and rocky, in the south-west there are splendid beaches of glistening shell sand set against machair lands and sheltered crofting communities.

Like much of western Scotland, especially the islands, Mull has seen its share of that shadowy period

in Scottish history known as 'the Clearances', but on Mull, the story of depopulation is not as clear-cut as elsewhere. Surprisingly, perhaps, for an island so close to mainland Scotland, Mull is relatively undeveloped, with few of the 'town' facilities and services of Oban. You come to Mull to escape and to enjoy its fundamental simplicity, for that is its charm. And the exploration of the winding narrow roads, all of them feeding into heathered and loch-filled glens, is the island's greatest pleasure.

As the eagle flies, Mull stretches 44.5km (28 miles) from Ardmore Point in the north to Rudh' Ardalanish in the south, and 49km (30 miles) from Duart Point in the east to the coast overlooking Iona in the west. But such statistics are meaningless in this contorted landscape. At its narrowest, Mull is a mere 4.25km (2½ miles) from Salen Bay to Killiechronan. Around the coast lie numerous islands, for Mull is not so much one island as an island group; some – Ulva, Gometra, Erraid and Iona – have interest for walkers. Others – Treshnish Isles and Staffa – are the stuff of legend, and popular on the tourist and wildlife trails. But Mull and its islands are not a place to be consumed in haste. Even visitors with the most basic interest in matters of natural history will find themselves stopping by the roadside to peer at seals, otters, deer, and the birds of the air.

It is a far cry from the scene that greeted Dr Johnson, who visited the island in October 1773, admittedly on a drab day, and remarked that Mull was 'a dreary country, much worse than Sky...a most dolorous country!'. His companion Boswell, however, seems to have been rather more discerning, describing the island as 'a hilly country, diversified with heath and grass, and many rivulets'.

Such opposing views of Mull may well be typical; much depends on the eye of the beholder. But even on the gloomiest of days, the beauty of Mull will out, and the rewards for patience and persistence are memories that will last a lifetime and a joy that will make the heart ache.

HISTORY

The history of Mull is not well documented, and there has been no attempt by anyone to write a full history of the island, except for a two-volume work by J P Maclean, published in America in 1922. Those volumes were essentially anthological, based on published works at the time and not on research in original material. Jo Currie's book *Mull: The Island and its People*, published in 2000, is excellent for detailed information about the history of the families and clans of the island (and its islands), but is not an authoritative treatise on island history. Numerous lesser publications

Standing stones, Glen Gorm (Walk 1.4)

and information on the internet give potted histories of Mull, but a definitive work by a professional historian is long overdue.

It is generally believed that Mull was first inhabited about 8000–10,000 years ago, following the last Ice Age. Hunter-gatherers lived in caves, such as the so-called Livingston's Cave on Ulva, and roamed freely across the island group. Then came the great transition, when the nomadic people started to settle down and become farmers, as they did throughout Britain and much of Europe, anything up to 6000 years ago. These Neolithic people, and the Bronze Age people that followed them, were responsible for many of the burial cairns that still dot the islands. Their presence is attested by a wealth of such cairns, cists, standing stones, stone circles, beaker pottery and knife blades. The Iron Age people who lived on Mull from around 2500–1500 years ago built forts, brochs, duns and crannogs, and a great many defensive settlements across the islands.

Christianity is believed to have come to the islands in the sixth century, when Columba landed from Ireland on the southernmost point of Iona, and set up a monastery on the island. But within a century, the island of Iona was sacked by Vikings, who continued to raid the islands of Mull for several centuries before becoming settlers.

In the 14th century, Mull became part of the Lordship of the Isles, but

after the collapse of the Lordship in 1493, the island was taken over by the Clan MacLean, who were to suffer for their support of the Royalist cause during the Commonwealth and later for their Jacobite tendencies. Their dispossessed lands were awarded to the Campbells, the Dukes of Argyll, and although they tried to encourage industry in Mull, without much success, financial problems forced them to part with their Mull lands by the mid-19th century.

The clan system, however, was always important, and following the end of the 15th century, virtually all the inhabitants lived within the clan system, a complex social hierarchy within which the clan chief held the land in trust for his clansmen, who were in turn bound to him in ties of kinship. This way of life was largely pastoral, founded on breeding cattle, which was the only form of wealth that could be liquidated by export to the mainland. Many of the routes taken by the cattle drovers across the island can still be followed today, virtually all of them leading to the lovely setting of Grasspoint near Craignure from where the beasts were taken to the island of Kerrera and onward to the mainland.

As with many of the Scottish islands, Mull suffered its share of grief under the so-called Highland Clearances, and it would be temptingly incorrect to assume that all the houses found derelict by the roadside are the by-product of the Clearances;

Tobermory

in fact, many of the houses were still inhabited in the 20th century. Evidence of the Clearances is, however, found all over the islands. Twenty crofters and three townships were cleared in Mishnish in the north of the island in 1842. Glengorm suffered hugely at the hands of James Forsyth, with wholesale clearances of crofts and townships. Four centres were cleared in Calgary in 1822, while in Treshnish three townships were cleared in 1862. Ulva and Gometra saw arguably the most extensive destruction when 100 people were evicted between 1846 and 1851, and were soon followed by the remaining inhabitants of the islands.

The main settlement on Mull today is Tobermory, which in 1788 was built by the British Fisheries Society, as a planned settlement.

Over the centuries Mull's population increased, reaching 10,638 in 1831, but the potato famine and then the Clearances rapidly reduced this number. By the 20th century much of the population had emigrated and there were more sheep on Mull than people.

Today Mull and its neighbouring islands have a population of fewer than 3000. Farming, fishing and forestry used to be the economic mainstays of the island, but increasingly, tourism is responsible for much of the island economy.

GEOLOGY

If the history of Mull is not very well documented, the island's geology is quite the opposite, and its geological pedigree is such that it has for many

Basalt columns, Ulva (Walk 4.1)

years attracted geologists in large numbers, who come to marvel at the landscape and its secrets. Common to most accounts is the imagery that Mull is constructed like a multi-tiered wedding cake, with thick layers of basalt lava sitting on top of a complicated basement of much older rocks which poke out around the edges of Mull. Geologists love Mull because it has such a long and interesting history (the oldest rocks, found on Iona, are about 2000 million years old), and it has unique structures and rocks found nowhere else in the world.

Like much of Britain, Mull has not always been in its present position, and geological time has seen it affected by enormous changes. Mull's oldest rocks were formed in the southern hemisphere, and, in common with the rest of the British Isles, Mull has

gradually drifted northwards. A study of its rocks, even by the non-specialist, shows that they have preserved details of the climatic zones that they passed through on their northward journey. One particularly fine example of this will be found if you stand on the shoreline opposite Inch Kenneth at Gribun. Here, you will be standing on sandstones deposited in a desert region at the same sort of latitude as the Persian Gulf.

Even the untrained eye can see that most of Mull is made of lava; the tell-tale flows ripple across the landscape virtually everywhere. The lava poured from volcanoes at a time when the north Atlantic was forming, and Mull was torn apart from its then neighbour Greenland as the vast super-continent which once joined North America and Europe divided.

The molten lava that erupted 50–60 million years ago, at intervals of thousands of years, forms Mull's stepped tablelands. Into these, intrusions of other rocks, all formed by fire, later took place, creating the mountains of Mull's central igneous complex, of which the Geological Survey of Scotland in 1924, said: 'Mull includes the most complicated igneous centre as yet accorded detailed examination anywhere in the world.' Volcanic explosions and intense earthquakes shook Mull throughout its formative years, and one of the old fault lines, the Great Glen Fault, which touches upon the southern part of Mull, is still occasionally active.

As with the rest of Britain, Mull's final shape was carved by glaciers that melted only 10,000 years ago, leaving behind deep U-shaped valleys between the mountains and long glaciated lochs. Of these, Glen Clachaig is a supreme example. It is a wild and fascinating landscape, made all the more intriguing by even a superficial understanding of what you are looking at. That glaciers were a part of Mull's geological profile is evidenced by the presence of isolated boulders, or erratics, that litter the landscape. Elsewhere, as at the head of Loch Scridain and Loch na Keal, you find the rocks have been heavily scored by the passage of ice-borne rocks. Once the glaciers were gone, the landscape that remained was little different from what you see today; in a sense it remains quite primeval, boasting a geological antiquity that is quite tangible and endlessly absorbing.

Glen Clachaig (Walk 2.6)

PLANTS AND WILDLIFE

For such a small island, Mull is amazingly diverse in its plant life, with more than 4000 different plant species. There are no less than 800 flowering plants and conifers, almost 250 different seaweeds, 56 ferns, 556 mosses and liverworts, almost 700 lichens and just under 1800 fungi... enough to keep even amateur botanists enthralled on every walk in this book, and for years to come.

First impressions are often misleading, for at times there is a prevailing sense of great swathes of bracken and heather. But that is only part of the story, and each season brings its own varieties, from the wild daffodils, bluebells, primroses and violets of spring to the winter deep greens; from the swaying foxgloves, orchids and harebells of summer to the gold of autumn. Wherever plants can grow, they do: Grass of Parnassus, tormentil, asphodel, scabious and cotton grass brighten the moorland bogs, while even the mountain peaks yield gentians and alpines.

There is much commercial forest on Mull, mainly featuring Sitka spruce, Japanese larch and lodgepole pine, but there is also an abundance of deciduous trees like birch, oak, rowan and wild cherry.

Nor is it all about the plants; the wildlife of these islands is every bit as varied. Red deer are seen almost anywhere and everywhere, with fallow deer populating the woodlands around Loch na Keal and Loch Ba. There are even wild goats, which keep very much to themselves among the coastal cliffs. Mull and Ulva have

Heather in bloom in Tireragan reserve (Walk 3.6)

Black highland bull

adders and slow worms, although neither are present on Iona.

Around the coast, you frequently see common seals and grey seals; dolphins, too, and whales are also often spotted, especially minke whales, harbour porpoises and bottlenose dolphins; on rare occasions you may be fortunate enough to spot killer whales (orca) and basking sharks. But perhaps more than any other form of wildlife, it is the otter that attracts most attention. Far from uncommon, they can be spotted around the waterline along the rocky shores or playing in the water a little further out; they even frequent the harbour at Tobermory. Patience usually brings its own rewards, although a number of businesses have developed to take visitors to favoured locations.

Golden eagles, sea eagles and buzzards are the island's most stunning birds of prey, but there are hen harrier, too, kestrel, merlin, short-eared owl, peregrine falcon and osprey. On the lochs, great northern divers often appear in winter, along with Slavonian grebe, barnacle and white-fronted geese, while the breeding season sees numbers of guillemot, puffin and gannet on and around the offshore islands.

WHEN TO GO

Mull is an island you can visit at any time of the year, and the walking is just as agreeable in winter as in summer, as long as you are appropriately skilled and experienced in venturing into the high mountains in winter.

For many, visitors and residents alike, Scotland's least appealing feature is the wee beastie known as the midge, which have been known to drive grown men to tears. These are out-and-about from June to September. So if you are susceptible to insect bites, it is wise to avoid these times, or take suitable precautions. They are at their worst in still, warm conditions. So any kind of breeze is to be welcomed!

HOW TO GET THERE

Oban is the main approach to Mull from the Scottish mainland and where the trains from Glasgow terminate.

By car and bus

The most popular route from Glasgow to Oban is 160km (100 miles) by Loch Lomond to Crianlarich, and then via Tyndrum, where the road to Oban (A85) branches left to Connel and then Oban. The route up the A82 beside Loch Lomond, however, is popular and busy, and some stretches await 'improvement', which many hope will never come.

There is an alternative approach for those with time to make a leisurely route, and this involves continuing along the M8 from Glasgow to Gourock and taking the half-hourly ferry (taking 20 minutes) across the Firth of Clyde to Dunoon. Then take the road around Loch Fyne to Inveraray and then north to Stronmilchan, there turning west to Oban. This route is 170km (105 miles).

For up-to-date driving information in the Highlands, call 0900 3401 363 (Highland Roadline), or 0900 3444 900 (The AA Roadline). For road-based journey planning, have a look at the AA or RAC Route Planners online.

Calmac ferry

Bus services to Oban are oper-
ated by Scottish Citylink Coaches Ltd.
(Buchanan Bus Station, Killermont
Street, Glasgow G2 3NW; tel: 08705
50 50 50; email: info@citylink.co.uk;
website: www.citylink.co.uk).

Travelling by car from the north,
there are two ways to Mull, either
via Oban, or by taking the Corran
ferry (south of Fort William) over
Loch Linnhe and across Morvern to
Lochaline, from where ferries cross to
Fishnish. Of use only to those already
exploring the Ardnamurchan peninsula, or those simply exploring, there
is a ferry from Kilchoan to Tobermory.

By rail

Virgin Trains operate from London and
stations in between to Glasgow via
the West Coast line – see www.virgin
trains.co.uk for more information.

The railway from Glasgow follows much of the same route as that
used by cars and buses, although the
early stages on leaving Glasgow differ
until you reach Tarbert.

For National Rail Enquiries, call
08457 48 49 50 (24 hours, seven days
a week). See also www.thetrainline.
com.

By ferry

Caledonian MacBrayne operates all
the ferry services running to Mull
(The Ferry Terminal, Gourock PA19
1QP; tel: 01475 650100; fax: 01475
637607; booking hotline: 08000 66
5000. You can book online at www.
calmac.co.uk.

Although there is an adequate bus
service across the island, exploring
Mull is best accomplished on foot, on
a bike, or by car. But it is important to
realise that most of the roads on Mull
are single track roads with passing
places. There are no urban motorways
here, no high-speed roads on which
it is safe to drive at high speeds, and
the only dual carriageway is brief and
single track, just south of Salen.

One of the continuing delights
of Mull is that you can achieve quite
significant circuits on its limited road
network but the limitations of the
roads make journeys longer than
might be expected. From Craignure
to Tobermory it is about 33km (21
miles), but it is a journey that will take
around 45 minutes; the road is good
as far as Salen, but then becomes single track. Craignure to Fionnphort is
56km (35 miles), a beautiful drive, but
one that will take at least an hour.

Cars are not permitted on Iona,
Ulva or Gometra. These islands are for
pedestrians, and getting there is easy.

Getting to Iona

Caledonian MacBrayne operates a
frequent service between Fionnphort
and Iona (tel: 01681 700559 or 01680
812343; website: www.calmac.co.uk).

Getting to Ulva and Gometra

Ulva is reached by a two-minute
crossing on demand – signal at the
pier. The ferry operates **from Easter to
the end of September**, Mon–Fri (and

Sun, June to August only), 9am–5pm, and **from the end of September to Easter**, Mon–Fri for the post and the school run only (call the boathouse (01688 500241) or the ferryman (01688 500226 or 07919 902407) the day before to confirm times).

Gometra can be reached by a bridge from Ulva, or by a direct, small, fast or semi-fast ferry on Loch Tuath (tel: 01688 500221 in the evening, or enquire at the tourist information office in Craignure).

Driving on Mull

Passing places are identified by either a white diamond or a black-and-white pole. These spaces serve two purposes: the first is to allow oncoming traffic to proceed; the other, often ignored, is to allow following vehicles to overtake. If a vehicle is following closely behind you must allow it to pass – it is an offence not to do so. But, always stop on the left when using passing places. If the passing place is on your right, wait opposite it to allow traffic to pass. You must not cross to the right; keep left. Following cars may be local tradesman going about their business; it is a courtesy to allow them to get on.

Driving slowly is not an issue, in any case there are few places where you can safely put your foot down. No-one minds how slowly you drive, as long as you let others pass; in fact, the slower you drive, the greater the likelihood of spotting something interesting. Do not park in passing

places, not even briefly; they are not viewpoints. Bear in mind, too, that the nature of the roads on Mull means that you will be doing a lot of slowing down and starting off again. This means increased wear and tear on brakes and tyres, as well as increased fuel consumption.

ACCOMMODATION

Tobermory is the main town, and offers a range of accommodation from hotels to guest houses, B&Bs and a youth hostel. Elsewhere, and generally across the whole island group, there are guest houses and B&Bs in good number. Camping and caravan sites are few and far between – see Appendix 3 for details. All main facilities are available in Tobermory, including the island's only static bank (the Royal Bank of Scotland has a mobile banking service). Elsewhere, the facilities are intended primarily for locals rather than visitors.

COMMUNICATIONS

Postal services are the same as for mainland Britain, but there is poor, limited and variable mobile phone coverage across much of the island.

There are very few places where you can connect to the internet, and such as there are will be found in Tobermory. Some hotels, however, do have wireless connections.

English is spoken everywhere; Gaelic hardly at all. Until within the

Walking along the raised beach, Treshnish (Walk 1.10)

last hundred years, however, Gaelic was the everyday language; today it is heard only among a small number of the older population. Yet, in Salen school, there is a Gaelic unit teaching children from three to 11 years old in Gaelic, and the Mull Gaelic Choir (Còisir Ghàidhlig an Eilein Mhuilich) is renowned throughout Scotland.

USING THIS GUIDE

Walking on Mull ranges from short and easy outings not far from civilisation, to rugged, hard mountain, moorland and coastal walking – as demanding as any in Britain – in isolated locations, where help is far away. Almost all of it demands a high level of fitness and knowledge of the techniques and requirements necessary to travel safely in wild countryside in very changeable weather conditions, including the ability to use map and compass properly.

The walks in this book are widely varied in character and will provide something for everyone, embracing high mountains, lonely lochs, coastal cliffs, glens and forests. Many walks visit places that are less well known, where self-sufficiency is critically important. But every walk is just that, a walk, and does not require rock climbing or scrambling skills beyond the most fundamental; ironically those skills are more likely to be tested along stretches of the rugged coastline than on the high mountains.

All parts of the island are visited, and the chosen walks will provide an excuse for many visits to the island, and allow walkers to evade inclement weather in one part of the island by taking on walks in another.

Each walk description begins with a short introduction, and provides

23

Ben More (Walk 2.9)

starting and finishing points, as well as a calculation of the distance and height gain, and an indication of the terrain which will be encountered. The walks are grouped largely within the generally recognised regions of Mull, and, within those areas, in a reasonably logical order.

Peak bagging

This book has not been written to facilitate peak bagging. But, for the record, Mull has just one Munro (Ben More), one Corbett and seven Grahams. If you collect Marilyns, then you have 27 to contend with on Mull and the adjacent islands, only 11 of which are included in the book. Information about the mountains database as it concerns Mull is found at www.mountaindays.net.

- Based on a list originally published in 1891 by Sir Hugh Munro, **Munros** are Scottish hills that are at least 3000ft (914m) in height and considered to be distinct and separate mountains.
- **Corbetts** are the range of Scottish hills beneath Munros. They are between 2500 and 2999ft (762–914m) high with a drop of 500ft (150m) on all sides.
- **Grahams** are Scottish hills between 2000 and 2499ft (609–762m) high with a drop of 500ft (150m) on all sides.
- **Marilyns** are British hills of any height with a drop of at least 150m on all sides.

Distances

Distances are given in kilometres (and miles), and represent the total distance for the described walk, that is from the starting point to the finishing point. Where a walk continues from a previously described walk, the distance given is the total additional distance involved. When a walk is to a single summit, the distance assumes a retreat by the outward route.

Total ascent

The figures given for ascent represent the total height gain for the complete walk, including the return journey, where appropriate. They are given in metres (and feet, nominally rounded up or down).

No attempt is made to grade walks, as this is far too subjective, and depends on abilities that vary from person to person, and, indeed, what they are accustomed to walking. But the combination of distance and total ascent should enable you to calculate roughly how long each walk will take using whatever method – Naismith's or other – you find works for you. On Mull, however, generous allowance must also be made on most walks for the ruggedness of the terrain and the possibility that any streams that must be crossed may prove awkward, or indeed completely impassable at the most convenient spot, necessitating long detours or even a retreat.

ACCESS IN SCOTLAND

Walkers in Scotland have always taken access by custom, tradition or right over most land and water in Scotland. This is now enshrined in the Land Reform (Scotland) Act 2003, which came into effect in February 2005. The Act tells you where rights of access apply, while the Scottish

Blàr Dubh, Ardalanish (Walk 3.5)

Outdoor Access Code sets out your responsibilities when exercising your rights. These responsibilities can be summarised as:

- take responsibility for your own actions
- respect the interests of other people, and
- care for the environment.

Access rights can be exercised over most land and inland water in Scotland by all non-motorised users, including walkers, cyclists, horse riders and canoeists, providing they do so responsibly. Walkers and others must behave in ways which are compatible with land management needs, and land managers also have reciprocal responsibilities to manage their land to facilitate access, taken either by right, custom or tradition. Local authorities and national park authorities have a duty and the powers to uphold access rights. People may be requested not to take access for certain periods of time when, for example, tree-felling is taking place, or for nature conservation reasons. It is responsible to comply with reasonable requests. Access rights also extend to lightweight, informal camping.

Access rights apply in places such as:

- hills, mountains and moorland
- woods and forests
- most urban parks, country parks and other managed open spaces
- rivers, lochs, canals and reservoirs

- riverbanks, loch shores, beaches and the coastline
- land in which crops have not been sown
- on the margins of fields where crops are growing or have been sown and along the 'tramlines' or other tracks which cross the cropped area
- grassland, including grass being grown for hay or silage (except when it is at such a late stage of growth that it is likely to be damaged)
- fields where there are horses, cattle and other farm animals
- on all core paths agreed by the local authority
- on all other paths and tracks where these cross land on which access rights can be exercised
- on grass sports or playing fields, when not in use, and on land or inland water developed or set out for a recreational purpose, unless the exercise of access rights would interfere with the carrying on of that recreational use
- golf courses, but only for crossing them and providing that you do not take access across greens or interfere with any games of golf
- on, through or over bridges, tunnels, causeways, launching sites, groynes, weirs, boulder weirs, embankments of canals and similar waterways, fences, walls or anything designed to

facilitate access (such as gates or stiles)

Farmyards are not included in the right of access, but you may still take access through farmyards by rights of way, custom or tradition. Farmers are encouraged to sign alternative routes if they do not want people passing through their farmyard. If you are going through a farmyard, proceed with care and respect the privacy of those living on the farm.

There have been a few, but not many, issues of access on Mull and Iona, always in the vicinity of farms. Most have to do with dogs not appropriately restrained. Please show due consideration when near farms; these are working environments, and a lack of understanding can generate difficulties for the people who manage and work the land.

Access rights do not apply to houses or other buildings, or to the immediate surrounding areas, including garden ground. Access rights apply to the woodland and grassland areas within the 'policies' of large estates but not to the mown lawns near the house.

The above is not a complete statement of the law as it applies in Scotland, and is no substitute for a comprehensive understanding of the situation. For more information and to download a copy of the Scottish Outdoor Access Code, see www. outdooraccess-scotland.com or www. ramblers.org.uk/scotland.

About dogs

Keep your dog under proper control:

- do not let it worry or attack livestock
- do not take it into a field where there are calves or lambs
- keep it on a short lead or under close control in fields where there are farm animals
- if cattle react aggressively and move towards you, keep calm, let the dog go and take the shortest, safest route out of the field
- keep it on a short lead or under close control during the bird breeding season (usually April to July) in areas such as moorland, forests, grassland, loch shores and the seashore and
- pick up and remove any faeces if your dog defecates in a public open place.

STALKING

Wild deer stalking is an essential part of the deer management programme, and takes place between July and February. Stalking does not occur on Sundays. Unlike, say, the Isle of Skye, Mull does not have a Hillphone system that you can call to check about stalking. You need to phone the relevant estate office.

Deer stalking occurs on a number of estates on Mull. The red deer stag stalking season runs from 1 July to 20 October; the red deer hind stalking season from 21 October to

The ridge to Dun da Ghaoithe from Mainnir nam Fiadh (Walk 2.14)

15 February. Locally these dates vary from one estate to the next, but given such a wide time span, it is a courtesy (at the least) and wisdom (at best) to check with the relevant estate offices (see Appendix 3) whether there is going to be any stalking in the areas you intend to visit.

Notices are sometimes posted at entrances to estate lands where stalking may be taking place, but this is not a requirement, not always done, not always possible and is not done consistently across the island. Do not presume that the absence of any such notices means that there is no stalking taking place; check!

SAFETY

The fundamentals of safety in the hills should be known by everyone heading for Mull intent on walking, but no apology is made for reiterating some basic dos and don'ts.

- Always take the basic minimum kit with you: sturdy boots, warm, windproof clothing, waterproofs (including overtrousers), hat or balaclava, gloves or mittens, spare clothing, maps, compass, whistle, survival bag, emergency rations, first aid kit, food and drink for the day, all carried in a suitable rucksack.
- Let someone know where you are going.

- Learn to use a map and compass effectively, and don't venture into hazardous terrain until you can.
- Make sure you know how to get a local weather forecast.
- Know basic first aid – your knowledge could save a life.
- Plan your route according to your ability, and be honest about your ability and expertise.
- Never be afraid to turn back.
- Be aware of your surroundings – keep an eye on the weather, your companions, and other people.
- Take extra care during descent.
- Be winter-wise – snow lingers in the corries well into summer. If snow lies across or near your intended route, take an ice axe (and the knowledge to use it properly).
- Have some idea of emergency procedures. As a minimum you should know how to call out a mountain rescue team (dial 999), and, from any point in your walk, know the quickest way to a telephone. You should also know something of the causes, treatment and ways of avoiding mountain hypothermia.
- Respect the mountain environment – be conservation minded.

On Mull it is vital to be properly equipped and to walk within your capabilities and experience; self-sufficiency is especially important here. There is no mountain rescue service on Mull – the nearest is in Oban. So,

the consequences of an accident may well be far worse than if rescue was closer to hand. Be well prepared.

In the event of an accident, telephone the police, but bear in mind, too, that mobile phone reception on Mull is neither extensive nor reliable.

MAPS

1:50,000
All the walks in this book can be found on the following Ordnance Survey Landranger Sheets:
- 47 Tobermory and North Mull
- 48 Iona and West Mull
- 49 Oban and East Mull.

1:25,000
Of greater use to walkers on Mull are Ordnance Survey Explorer maps, and for the whole of Mull you will need the following sheets:
- 373 Iona, Staff and Ross of Mull
- 374 Isle of Mull North and Tobermory
- 375 Isle of Mull East: Craignure.

All OS maps are all available from www.ordnancesurvey.co.uk.

PATHS

Not all the paths mentioned in the text appear on maps. And where they do, there is no guarantee that they still exist on the ground, remain continuous or well defined.

A number of the walks go close to the top of dangerous cliffs, both coastal and inland. Here the greatest care is required, especially in windy conditions. Do not, for any reason, venture close to cliff tops. Some of the routes rely on sheep tracks, which make useful paths in otherwise trackless areas. Sheep, however, do not appear to suffer from vertigo, and don't travel about with awkward, laden sacks on their backs. If a track goes towards a cliff, avoid it, and find a safer, more distant, alternative. Burns should be crossed at the most suitable (and safest) point, which can involve lengthy, and higher, detours in spate conditions. Do not allow the frustrations of such a detour to propel you into attempting a lower crossing against your better judgement.

If there are children in your party, keep them under close supervision and control at all times.

With only a small but growing number of exceptions, paths are not waymarked or signposted. Many of the mountain paths, however, are cairned. In a constantly developing environment like Mull, changes often occur to routes, especially through forests (where trees are felled), or on coastal walks (as a result of landslip, for example). See the Advice to Readers box at the front of the book for information about how to let Cicerone know of any changes that you come across for the benefit of future walkers.

The path around the Calgary headland (Walk 1.9)

1 NORTH MULL

INTRODUCTION

The north of Mull boasts little in the way of significant upland; the highest point, Speinne Mòr, rises to a mere 444m (1456ft). But what it does have is a bounty of coastal walking – some of the finest on the island – and quite an array of woodland and moorland walks. There are only two important settlements here – Tobermory and Dervaig – three if you include Salen, which sits on the arbitrary boundary between north and central Mull.

A goodly proportion of north Mull is forested, although clearing is currently an on-going feature, but there is also a great swathe of open moorland, generally of the most demanding kind where only experienced walkers should venture away from the established paths and trails.

South of Tobermory lies the area known as Aros, while to the north and west are Mishnish and Quinish respectively, where the tell-tale signs of lava bedrock ripple away into the distance. What makes this region of Mull especially appealing is the convoluted nature of the terrain; this is a hummocky, undulating, twisted landscape of considerable beauty, bringing new vistas at almost every step and exposing the visitor to enticing views of surrounding islands, Coll and Tiree, and the mainland fastnesses of Morvern and Ardnamurchan.

Further west, headland points like Caliach and Treshnish, especially the latter, provide some of the finest walking on Mull, where interest is constantly maintained and the evidence

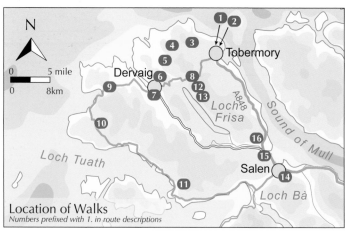

Location of Walks
Numbers prefixed with 1. in route descriptions

Rainbow over Eileanan Glasa

of past ways of life litter the landscape and raise their tumbled remains above the encroaching bracken and heather.

North Mull is for walkers rather than mountaineers, and provides considerable scope to invent walks and pit yourself against the ruggedness of the land, where navigation skills need to be of the highest order. Many walks described in this book take you far away from outside help, and so the ability to self-help in rugged terrain is of paramount importance. In return, you will be rewarded with days of solitude and tranquillity where eagles dare and otters make the most of the coast and inland lochs.

WALK 1.1

Tobermory and Aros Park

Start/Finish	Tobermory car park (NM505551)
Distance	5.5km (3½ miles)
Total ascent	90m (295ft)
Terrain	Woodland and lakeside paths
Map	OS Explorer 374 Isle of Mull North and Tobermory

Aros Park is a green lung for Tobermory, not that it needs it, given the breezy ozone that permanently mantles the town. But this sometime estate park, now owned by the Forestry Commission, is linked to Tobermory for good reason: it is the perfect place to explore a managed estate woodland, to enjoy the ornamental lake carpeted with water lilies, and to harvest a bounty of brambles in season. The woodlands are rich and lush with ash, rowan, hazel, birch, beech, oak and various pine, as well as rhododendron, a tell-tale sign of a managed estate. Thick layers of moss cloak many of the trees, both living and long-since felled, while the understorey has a fine range of fungi later in the year. This walk is straightforward and uncomplicated.

Leave the car park by setting off along a path near the pub (signed 'Coastal Path to Aros Park'), climbing a little at the end of a cliff, then going forward along a terraced path with the sea down below to your left. Throughout the walk there are stands of oak, beech, birch, hazel, alder, rowan and a few lime.

Spùt Dubh (Black Spout), as its name suggests, is a waterfall, a once-important supply of fresh, albeit peat-stained, water for ships in years gone by. Beyond that, a landslide some years ago necessitated a little re-routing, but the path maintains a steady course above the waters of Tobermory Bay, with Calve Island riding at anchor offshore, protecting the Tobermory harbour from east winds.

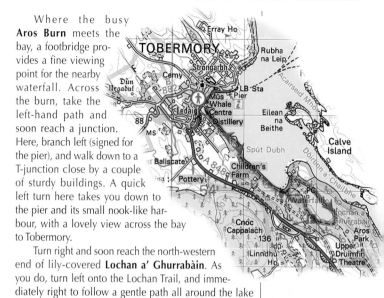

Where the busy **Aros Burn** meets the bay, a footbridge provides a fine viewing point for the nearby waterfall. Across the burn, take the left-hand path and soon reach a junction. Here, branch left (signed for the pier), and walk down to a T-junction close by a couple of sturdy buildings. A quick left turn here takes you down to the pier and its small nook-like harbour, with a lovely view across the bay to Tobermory.

Turn right and soon reach the north-western end of lily-covered **Lochan a' Ghurrabàin**. As you do, turn left onto the Lochan Trail, and immediately right to follow a gentle path all around the lake through mature woodland. At the far end of the lake, the path divides. Branch right, and, just on crossing a simple footbridge spanning a stream (with a dilapidated pump house nearby) flowing from the distant Lochan na Guailne Duibhe away to the south-east, keep right, still on the Lochan Trail.

When the path next divides, take the left-hand branch, walking up to a large car park and picnic area. This spot may be reached more directly – to effect a shorter walk, or for that matter a picnic – by leaving the A848 at NM509541, at Aros Lodge.

The car park is the site of **Aros House**, owned by the Allan family, shipowners from Liverpool, who were resident here from 1874 until 1959. The gardens were planted by Alexander Allan, who tended the estate with great care and lived the life of a respectable country gentleman. By the 1950s, the estate had become a financial drain, and the Forestry Commission bought

35

*Lochan a' Ghurrabàin,
Aros Park*

the land but had no use for the house, which was sold on and later stripped of its oak panelling and lead roofing. In time, left as a shell, the house became a danger and the army demolished it in 1962.

Cross the car park, heading towards a small toilet block, just past which you find another path taking you back among the trees. This path, too, soon divides. Go left, climbing gently, and quickly arrive at a T-junction with the Aros Burn a few strides in front of you, and the lower **waterfall** and footbridge a short distance down to your right. If you want to extend the walking a little, then at the T-junction you can turn left and walk up beside the burn, crossing a main trail, and continuing to the upper waterfall. There are linking paths to get you back on line, but the simplest expedient is to return to the lower waterfall.

Cross the footbridge, and retrace your steps to **Tobermory**.

WALK 1.2

Rubha nan Gall

Start/Finish	Tobermory car park (NM505551)
Distance	5.2km (3¼ miles)
Total ascent	180m (590ft)
Terrain	Woodland paths across steep slope; golf course
Map	OS Explorer 374 Isle of Mull North and Tobermory

The brightly coloured houses of Tobermory are a delightful prelude to this mainly woodland walk to the lighthouse at Rubha nan Gall, the Headland of the Stranger. Although you can simply return the same way, there is an agreeable alternative that climbs up onto the headland and then treks around the edge of Tobermory's lumpy but beautiful golf course.

Tobermory, the main town on Mull, takes its name from the well and chapel of St Mary, although no-one seems to know precisely where (somewhere below the cemetery) the well is located. What remains of the chapel is found in the old part of the cemetery. The town was established in 1788 by the British Fisheries Society, although fishing never prospered here, in spite of the sheltered nature of the bay.

Walk to the far end of Tobermory, to the ferry point, and look for a path rising on the left just after the last building. This climbs easily, and soon wanders into light woodland, and then by a generally level path through a tunnel of trees around the edge of the bay.

At NM511565, the track divides. You will return to this point, but for now bear right and follow an improving, but sometimes muddy, path that suddenly breaks free of the woodland. Now, cross a steep slope covered with

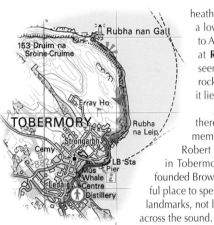

heather, bracken, gorse and birch, with a lovely view across the Sound of Mull to Ardnamurchan. Soon, the lighthouse at **Rubha nan Gall** comes into view, seemingly hunkered down among the rocks, until you get closer and see that it lies at the end of a small pier.

Just before reaching the light, there are steps on the right down to a memorial viewpoint, commemorating Robert John Brown, who lived close by in Tobermory, and whose father, Archibald, founded Browns shop in Tobermory. This is a useful place to spend a few minutes identifying distant landmarks, not least the squat triangle of Ben Hiant across the sound.

Press on along a clear path to reach the former lighthouse keepers' cottages at Rubha nan Gall and the lighthouse, first lit in 1857, and automated in the 1960s. Going further, beyond the light, takes you into difficult terrain, and is not advised.

Lighthouse, Rubha nan Gall

Tobermory

Northwards lies so-called **Bloody Bay**, where in 1480 a great sea battle took place between John, the last Lord of the Isles, and his son Angus. On that day the tide came ashore red with blood. And, as Jim Crumley explains in *The Heart of Mull*, so it is that the oyster-catcher owes its red beak and legs to its forebears who waded along the shore on that fateful day.

Retrace your steps to the point where the path divided, and there turn right, climbing easily through the woodland to reach its upper rim at an iron fence stanchion. Here turn left, pursuing a pleasant path above the upper limit of the woodland, undulating gently upwards through bracken to reach a step-stile at the edge of Tobermory **golf course**.

Cross the stile and keep left, following the manicured edges of the golf course, a splendid experience when stray golf balls are not flying in your direction. Keep on, with lovely views of Calve Island, until a path takes you away from the course edge, descending for a while, but then emerging back onto the golf course edge. Continue beyond the fifth green, and then ultimately the fifth tee, after which a path leads to an iron gate in a corner.

Through the gate you enter a neck of woodland, and in a few strides turn left to follow a clear path round the edge of Bad-Daraich house to a road head at **Oakfield** (NM509555). Now turn left, and when you reach the **war memorial**, turn left beside it, taking a descending path and steps that lead to the path used at the start of the walk. Turn right to return to the edge of Tobermory at the Calmac pier.

SUNKEN TREASURE

Those who enjoy a good yarn may find appeal in the story that an Armada galleon carrying untold treasure was destroyed close by the pier in 1588, and that great wealth, if you can find it, lies deep in the silt of the bay. There are numerous versions of the story, and of the 'detail' of how the galleon was blown up just as it was readying to sail. The most charming is that the Witch of Lochaber, engaged by Lady Maclean of Duart Castle to retrieve her husband from the attentions of a beautiful Spanish princess on board the galleon, called up an army of fairy cats, which swam out and savaged the crew. One, in pursuing a sailor, set off loose powder in the magazine with sparks from its fur, and so destroyed the galleon. While there can be little doubt that such a tale is perfectly true, Alison MacLeay gives an alternative version in *The Tobermory Treasure*, to which contemporary thinking ascribes greater veracity. The wreck was long thought to have been the man-of-war, the *Florencia*, but was, in fact, a Mediterranean carrack, the *San Juan de Sicilia*.

Ardmore Bay

WALK 1.3

Ardmore

Start/Finish	Ardmore forest car park (NM485558)
Distance	12km (7½ miles)
Total ascent	415m (1360ft)
Terrain	Forest trails; some narrow woodland paths; short stretch of coastal path
Map	OS Explorer 374 Isle of Mull North and Tobermory

Ardmore is the name of a lost village, buried beneath trees during afforestation in the 20th century. Nearby Penalbanach suffered the same fate, but now that the forest is being cleared, fern-clad, roofless dwellings are re-appearing to remind modern visitors that people once lived here. The plantation that remains is predominantly Sitka spruce and Japanese larch, but large swathes of it have been felled so that the whole walk is nothing like so enclosed or gloomy as might be expected. The walk concludes with a long stretch on a minor road, but one that passes through a pleasing landscape. Almost all of the route is potentially shared with cyclists.

The easiest of starts sets off from the forest car park, heading along a broad trail with mature trees on the left and an open, hillocky prospect on the right decorated with ling and bell heather. After about 800m, the track begins to descend gently, and ahead you can pick out the profile of Ben Hiant on the Ardnamurchan peninsula.

The on-going trail leads through a large cleared area with fine seaward views to South Uist and Barra in the Outer Hebrides skimming low and blue along the far horizon.

At NM476573, the track divides. Here bear right, following a route waymarked with red-banded poles. After a brief, gentle rise, the track begins a long and steady

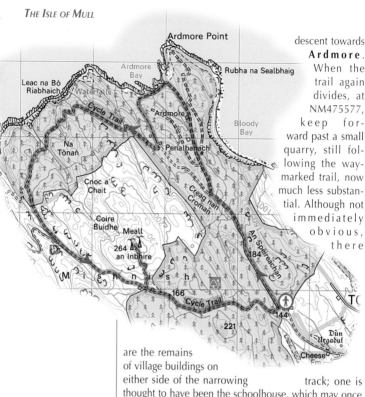

descent towards **Ardmore**. When the trail again divides, at NM475577, keep forward past a small quarry, still following the waymarked trail, now much less substantial. Although not immediately obvious, there are the remains of village buildings on either side of the narrowing track; one is thought to have been the schoolhouse, which may once have resounded to the cacophony of young voices.

The path curls downwards to cross the **Allt na Criche** on stepping stones that can sometimes be submerged, necessitating one giant leap for mankind, or a little paddling. Beyond, you re-enter plantation, among which more ruins of Ardmore appear; today, these are coated with ferns, mainly spleenwort, a poignantly attractive sight.

Eventually, the path leads you down pleasantly to arrive at **Ardmore Bay**, across which the island of Coll lies to the left. The path now swings left to follow the shoreline, its rocks displaying fine spreads of lava. A picnic table at NM468586 is a perfect spot from which to contemplate Ardmore Bay and indulge in a little sea-watching. Further on, beyond a footbridge, you reach a small hide where patience may be rewarded with sightings of seals, otters or passing eagles.

Continue past the hide and follow the path as it climbs steadily through spruce, and then through a cleared area to pass the derelict cottages at **Penalbanach**, one with a substantial rowan tree now protruding from where the roof should be. Just beyond, you join a broad forest trail, and turn right. If you turn left at this point, it will take you directly back to the start, thereby reducing the overall distance to 7km (4½ miles).

The track climbs steadily to round the northern end of Mishnish, and continues for a while enclosed by mature trees, but does then eventually break free and offers a pleasing view southwards to 'S Airde Beinn (see Walk 1.8). After a gate you finally leave the trees behind, with the path pressing on though bracken to reach a car park and surfaced road.

Initially beside the **Allt an Tairbh**, keep forward along the road, which will now guide you back to the start over a distance of 3.5km (2 miles). The road climbs gently at

The summit of Meall an Inbhire

first, as far as the turning to the radio masts on Meall an Inbhire, after which it undulates in a generally downwards direction back to the start.

If time permits, it is worth walking up the concrete service road to the wireless station on the summit of **Meall an Inbhire** (also known as Cnoc Fuar). ◄ This modest extension can be completed in a mere 20 minutes or so, and will add 1.4km (1 mile) and 70m (230ft) of height gain to the overall walk.

The road section back to the start is, as road walking goes, quite agreeable, its twists and turns bringing changing vistas of forest, purpled, heathery outcrops, neat ravines and distant landscapes, principally eastwards towards Morvern and Ardnamurchan, all of which contrive to enliven the final stages of the walk.

This summit isn't a Munro, a Corbett, or a Marilyn, but it is a stunning viewpoint looking west to Coll, north to Rum and east to Ardnamurchan; it also looks down on the trail just followed.

WALK 1.4

Glengorm Castle and Dùn Ara

Start/Finish	Glengorm car park (NM442571)
Distance	4km (2½ miles)
Total ascent	100m (320ft)
Terrain	Managed farmland; rocky headland; good path throughout
Map	OS Explorer 374 Isle of Mull North and Tobermory

Glengorm is a fairly modern name given to a part amalgamation of farms around Sorne and Quinish conveyed to James Forsyth in the 1840s. This out-and-back walk is brief but beautiful, and saunters across rugged pastureland to the small fort, known as Dùn Ara, perched on a hilltop overlooking the sea. It is the kind of place you could linger for many hours, sea watching, or for the intrepid, taking a dip in the bathing pool constructed nearby for those staying at the mansion during the time that it was owned by the Lithgow family.

From the car park, walk towards the café and gallery and cross the bridge directly opposite to follow a broad path flanked by hazel, fuchsia, rowan and rhododendron, soon breaking out into a sloping pasture with a fine seaward view. Follow the on-going path across improved, undulating farmland, with **Glengorm Castle** high above you on the left.

GLEN GORM

The origins of the name 'Glen Gorm' are uncertain, although folklore has an attractive offering. When James Forsyth began to build his mansion, he proposed to call it Dunara, after the coastal fort nearby. But he was advised that as the fort was a good mile away, to call his mansion after it was inappropriate. So, he is said to have consulted an old woman, who, with the recent and bitter memory of the clearances rained down on the estate by the same James Forsyth, suggested he called the mansion Glengorm, meaning 'blue glen'. The laird was delighted with the name, but how would he have responded had he realised that in putting forward the name, the old woman was actually commemorating a time when the glen was indeed blue, with the smoke from the townships he had put to the torch.

Maybe it was the same old woman, who died in 1917 having lived to see her 94th birthday, who passes down the tale that as the building of the house neared completion, Forsyth came to inspect its progress, but, as the door was opened to welcome him, a bat flew out and hit him in the face. His companions advised that the bat represented the soul of one of those evicted from his land, that it was a curse, and that he would never sleep in the house. He never did; shortly after this incident he was taken ill, and died before the house was finished.

The track leads to a gate beyond which it proceeds through a landscape of hummocks and hollows, all gently tilting towards the sea. A short way beyond the gate, the track forks. Branch right to intercept a more prominent track. Off to the left at this point, three standing stones within a circular outline of stones, can be seen, and are worth a brief visit.

Dùn Ara, Glen Gorm

Return to the main track, to a low waymark, and then follow a straight line through gates until the path, clear throughout, finally swings left to a final gate. **Dùn Ara** is atop the second prominent upthrust that you reach, and is accessed from a signpost via a narrow rocky gully.

Like all such coastal forts, **Dùn Ara** occupies a key defensive position, and may well have been built by the MacKinnons who controlled the lands of Sorne until the 17th century. The remains of several buildings can be discerned on the neat summit, along with more buildings below, and basic cultivation ridges known as a runrig. At the water's edge, obvious construction has been carried out to fashion a harbour and a small jetty. Local tradition relates that this was modified to become a bathing pool for the Lithgow family during their time in residence at Glengorm Castle.

It used to be possible to fashion a circular walk from Dùn Ara, by way of nearby Dùn Ban, back to Glengorm, but the introduction of fencing, some of it electrified, makes this now impossible. So, simply retrace your steps.

WALK 1.5

Loch an Torr and Glen Gorm

Start/Finish	Loch Frisa car park (NM463522)
Distance	10.2km (6½ miles)
Total ascent	255m (835ft)
Terrain	Forest trails; moorland tracks
Map	OS Explorer 374 Isle of Mull North and Tobermory

The forest of Quinish lies at the northern tip of Mull, and its wide trails, cleared in parts, provide walking that is protected from the worst of the elements, but without pressing in on the trail. In fact, Quinish forest has a number of gaps in its profile, through which views of the northern coastline and islands further afield can be glimpsed. This walk begins through the forest to the west of Loch an Torr, but in its second half breaks free of the trees to enjoy a leisurely amble on a good track across hummocky moorland. There are excellent tracks throughout, and the walking is of the easiest kind, with great spotted woodpeckers among the trees and the occasional snipe out on the moors.

Set off from the Loch Frisa car park by turning left along the road and walking as far as the branching track on the right (1.3km/¾ mile) signed for Loch Torr. Leave the road here to enter the forest of Quinish, and soon pass through a gate and then by a small quarry, shortly after which the trail divides. Branch left, climbing up to the forest edge, where the trail swings left, and continues climbing gently.

Loch Torr is little more than a hundred years old. Where it now lies used to be the confluence of two burns that combined to become Mingary Burn, encountered later in the walk. In 1899, the adjoining landowners decided to build a dam across the western end of what is now

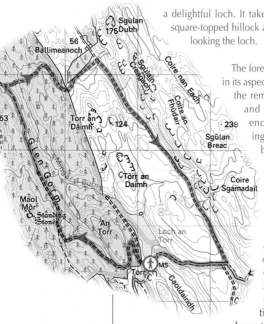

a delightful loch. It takes its name from the square-topped hillock above the road, overlooking the loch.

The forest is gratifyingly open in its aspect, and in a few places the remains of old cottages and farm buildings are encountered, projecting from the mantle of bracken like ribs on a hungry cow.

The track presses on to pass a larger quarry, and then crosses an open area allowing views across Ardnamurchan to the distant island of Rum. At NM432548 you reach a track junction, and should here leave the main forest trail by descending to the right onto another track (signed for Loch Frisa).

The trail leads down to cross the **Mingary Burn** by a footbridge beneath which the burn flows sedately through the centre of **Glen Gorm** en route to Loch Mingary. In days of old, this was the boundary between the Marches of Mingary and Glen Gorm. On the other side of the bridge, walk around the edge of a cleared area to land on another broad forest trail at a bend. Bear left, and walk on until suddenly at a deer gate (NM440548), you finally leave the forest and continue on a broad track across rough heath, which soon opens up into a wide valley below low cliffs.

On the far side of the valley, with the cottage of **Ballimeanoch** off to the left, you reach a junction. Leave the main track, which swings left to the cottage, by

Loch an Torr

bearing right onto a track for Loch Frisa. Soon you reach a gate after which the track continues across bracken slopes and a lovely hummocky landscape.

A shallow ford at NM458533 below a waterfall issuing from **Coire Sgamadail** is the only obstacle of note as you walk back towards the road. At NM461528, the track divides three ways. Take the middle option, passing through a gate and taking a clear path, descending to the road opposite the turning to the Loch Frisa **car park**.

WALK 1.6
Quinish Point and Mingary Aird

Start/Finish	Dervaig (NM430517)
Distance	13km (8 miles)
Total ascent	175m (575ft)
Terrain	Forest trails; open moorland; coastal pastures
Map	OS Explorer 374 Isle of Mull North and Tobermory

Mingary Aird is a small hill overlooking Quinish Point, and including it in this walk is a modest undertaking that will increase the overall distance by 500m, and the height gain by 50m (165ft). The Point itself is host to two duns, sites of ancient coastal forts: Dun Bàn and Dun Dubh, the White Fort and the Black Fort.

This out-and-back walk begins through the Quinish forest, and for the first hour is easy going; then a change of direction takes you into the forest and conditions that are for a while boggy. But this is short lived, and should deter no one. Suddenly, you pop out (ooze out might be a better expression after rain) of the forest, and cross brackeny heath to the isolated holiday cottage at Mingary before pressing on to the lonely headland at Quinish Point.

Start near the church in Dervaig and walk up the road towards Tobermory, passing the **Bellachroy Hotel** and the turning into Dervaig's main street, and continue climbing as far as a lane just before the Tobermory road sign, and here branch left to pass cottages, the first of which is **Sligachan**.

Follow the lane to enter the Quinish forest, and press on a little further to a parking area by a deer gate, which is an alternative starting point (NM433523) that would shorten the walk a little. Beyond the gate the forest trail rises steadily through an area of forest that has been cleared and allows views over Dervaig to the road winding across the hillside to Calgary, and of the undulating, knolly countryside around the forest.

The track eventually curves round to an indistinct junction at NM431549, where a stony track on the left leaves the main forest trail, as it sweeps away to the right. Do not confuse this turning with another a few strides further on (NM432548, and visible), used in Walk 1.5. Branch left, the track now less substantial than the main forest trail, but running on agreeably along the edge of plantation.

Stay with the track when it swings left at a firebreak. For a while the route continues as a rough vehicle track, in and out of plantation and through clearings. Finally, the track degenerates to a path through bracken at a clearing, but soon returns to the cover of the trees, crunching along on a pine needle carpet, but at times dancing around a few minor boggy bits.

Eventually, one final squelchy section leads you out of the forest to a gate; take great care not to slip here. Follow a path beyond through bracken to a small cairn on a low hillock, where the idyllically set holiday cottage at **Mingary** comes into view. Walk towards the cottage, and go through a gate in front of it, then cross to another at the left-hand edge of the building.

A broad grassy track leads away from the cottage and curls round a low hill, bringing another gate into view. Before the gate, however, turn right, on a clear, grassy path that runs arrow-straight into a low, wide valley. You can also reach the valley by turning immediately right after the cottage.

DERVAIG AND THE SMALLEST THEATRE IN THE WORLD

Dervaig is one of the most attractive villages in the Hebrides, and was built originally by Maclean of Coll in 1799, with 26 houses in pair, each with a sizeable garden and vital grazing rights (known as soumings) on common land, and intended to be a hive of industry. In 1857, the new landlord, James Forsyth (who built Glengorm Castle), induced the people of Dervaig to sign new leases, but failed to mention that they were for the house and garden only, not the grazing rights. Without those rights the tenants, who had trusted Forsyth, were reduced to living on what little they could grow in their gardens.

Until recent times, Dervaig was the location of the charming Mull Little Theatre, which seated fewer than 40. The theatre began life as the 'Thursday Theatre', an entertainment for guests at Druimard Guest House. It was built from the remains of an old cowshed in 1963, and grew in reputation to become the smallest professional theatre in the world.

The company dropped the 'little' from its name and became simply Mull Theatre. The final curtain at the original Little Theatre fell in 2006, and a new Centre opened in July 2008 at Druimfin, just outside Tobermory. Mull Theatre is funded by the Scottish Arts Council in recognition of its importance in touring its productions throughout Scotland.

Both duns are easily accessible, and on a fine day this is a lovely and tranquil location to be savoured before starting the return.

The path now runs all the way to **Quinish Point**, passing through a gate and below a line of low cliffs on the way, but wide and clear until finally the double-dunned headland comes into view. It's quite a special moment, the landscape largely carpeted with bracken, but with a few squares of lazybed (ridge-and-furrow pattern) still clearly seen. ◄

Walk back up the path, from which, at a point of your choosing, you can walk up easily through bracken to the trig pillar on the summit of **Mingary Aird**.

Return to the main path, and then retrace your steps to Mingary cottage, and then back through the forest.

Note: The intention was that this out-and-back walk would be circular, but at the time of writing (July 2010), there are unresolved access issues. If these are resolved in a way that allows the circular walk to be introduced, details will appear on the Cicerone website, and then in future editions of the book.

Quinish Point

WALK 1.7

Quinish, Glen Gorm and Ardmore

Start	Dervaig (NM430517)
Finish	Ardmore forest car park (NM485558); or Tobermory
Distance	Ardmore forest car park 15.5km (9¾ miles); Tobermory 18km (11¼ miles). Detour via villages adds 1.8km (1 mile)
Total ascent	Forest car park 585m (1920ft); Tobermory 600m (1970ft). Detour via villages adds 100m (330ft) of ascent
Total descent	Forest car park 450m (1475ft); Tobermory 610m (2000ft). Detour via villages adds 100m (330ft)
Terrain	Mainly broad forest trails; some road walking
Map	OS Explorer 374 Isle of Mull North and Tobermory

Spending much of its time in open forest, where the mature trees stand well back from the trails to allow pleasant glimpses of distant hills and islands, this walk, while lengthy, is quite easy. There is scope for breaking the walk at a little over half-way by diverting to the tea room at Glengorm Castle for refreshment before resuming. Walkers wanting to finish the walk in Tobermory can get to the start in Dervaig by using the local bus service; it's a lovely ride across the island, past the Mishnish lochs. A finish at the Ardmore car park needs either two cars or someone to drop you off in Dervaig and wait for you at the other end.

The walk is very much one of peaceful solitude, wandering quietly through the trees from which, in the cleared areas, the remains of ruined villages, like Penalbanach and Ardmore, are starting to re-appear. A pair of binoculars are also useful, as the forest has a good range of birdlife.

The road travelled is known locally as the Dervaig Back Road, a link with Tobermory that avoids the steepness and hairpins of the present-day B-road. As good a place as any to start is the church in Dervaig, overlooking Loch a' Chumhainn (Loch Cuan), close by the Glen Aros road to Salen. Here, stay on the B-road, heading towards Tobermory, but leaving it at the Tobermory road sign for a lane on the left, passing cottages to enter the **Quinish forest** (this is the same start as Walk 1.6). If you are being dropped off, you can drive along this lane and along a rough track to a deer gate by a pumping station.

The way through the forest is never in doubt, and leads easily to a junction with a path on the left (the second of two – the first is used by Walk 1.6) at NM432548. Signposts here point out the track for Loch Frisa that descends, with trees much closer now, to the **Mingary Burn**, crossed by an ancient footbridge. Go around the edge of the cleared area beyond, and soon reach another broad forest trail at a bend. Turn left, and follow this trail until, quite suddenly, you pop out of the forest at a deer gate (NM440548). Keep forward beyond the gate, crossing a wide, shallow valley of hummocks and hollows, and on the far side, stay with the track as it swings left towards the cottage of **Ballimeanoch**.

Walk on past the cottage, as far as a junction at NM439562, and there turn right to pass **Sorne cottages** to the narrow road serving Glengorm Castle. ▶

Turn right along the road, and follow it through a mildly convoluted landscape until you reach a car park for the **Ardmore Estate** (NM455566). Turn left here, leaving the road and walking forward through a gate. The trail is initially open and leads across heather moorland until it finally slips into mature forest. Now more forest trail walking ensues; it is easy and never in doubt, and leads by a serpentine route to a junction with a path on the left at NM469578. Press on past this, following the broad trail, and this will lead you unerringly to the Ardmore car park.

The continuation to **Tobermory** simply follows the road to a junction at NM498552. Either of the roads on the left will take you back in to Tobermory, although that on the right (for Salen) has less potential for confusion.

Walkers wishing to visit the tea room should turn left here, and then return.

Penalbanach, Ardmore

55

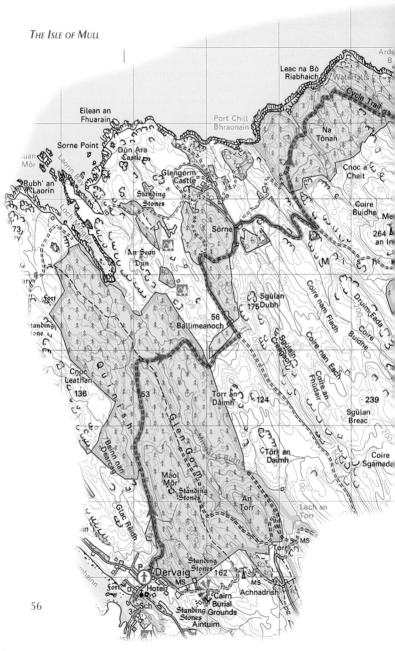

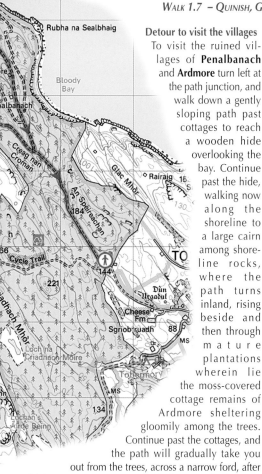

Detour to visit the villages

To visit the ruined villages of **Penalbanach** and **Ardmore** turn left at the path junction, and walk down a gently sloping path past cottages to reach a wooden hide overlooking the bay. Continue past the hide, walking now along the shoreline to a large cairn among shoreline rocks, where the path turns inland, rising beside and then through mature plantations wherein lie the moss-covered cottage remains of Ardmore sheltering gloomily among the trees. Continue past the cottages, and the path will gradually take you out from the trees, across a narrow ford, after which you soon revert to a wide forest trail. There are more ruins of Ardmore scattered about either side of the ford, but they are not always obvious. Follow the broad track forward (now waymarked with red-banded poles), and continue uneventfully to the **Ardmore** car park.

WALK 1.8
'S Airde Beinn and Crater Loch

Start/Finish	B8073, near old cottage, opposite Loch Meadhoin (NM476527)
Distance	3.2km (2 miles)
Total ascent	158m (520ft)
Terrain	Boggy moorland path through heather; moderately rocky rim of volcanic vent
Map	OS Explorer 374 Isle of Mull North and Tobermory

Very little expenditure of energy will be needed to conquer this Marilyn; it succumbs quite readily. But its status among peak-baggers is not the only reason for visiting 'S Airde Beinn, the High Hill. This minor summit is what remains of a volcanic vent, within which now reposes a lovely loch, and the gentle walk to it across heather moorland is quite agreeable, if woefully brief. Yet for such a lowly height, 'S Airde Beinn dominates the surrounding landscape of Mishnish, and provides excellent views northwards to the Ardnamurchan peninsula and the Small Isles, and north-east over Tobermory Bay into the maw of Loch Sunart, which separates Ardnamurchan from the ruggedness that is Morvern.

Beside the ruined cottage, close by the point where Loch Meadhoin and Loch Carnain an Arnais meet, there is room to park a couple of cars clear of the nearby passing place. Cross a low step-stile, and take to a clear path rising easily through bracken to a gate. Beyond the gate, the terrain becomes wet heather moorland, with the southern edge of **'S Airde Beinn** rising ahead.

This modest hill is all that remains of a lesser volcanic vent that during the Tertiary Age (50–60 million years ago) issued huge quantities

of molten rock and ash, building up the foundations of Mull, which were later eroded to their present state.

The path wanders boggily across the moor, bringing ever-widening views of considerable delight. Walk on steadily until the path divides at NM473533. Here bear left, and climb a little more steeply to gain the rim of the crater, from which you gaze down on **Lochan 'S Airde Beinn**, known locally as Crater Loch. The moment is quite special, and you half expect to see visiting whooper swans or cavorting otters on the loch, which indeed is a sight that will greet some fortunate visitor. With that possibility in mind, and given the simple beauty of the location, there is much to be said for bringing your lunch with you, and spending a few hours hunkered down among the rocks. ▶

Once on the rim, bear left and ascend easily to a cairn on a boulder that marks the highest point of this peak, and take a few moments to appreciate the view. Then continue round the rim; the path leads on, and is straightforward and clear throughout, circling round to the eastern side of the lake and then descending to cross a boggy patch before passing through a collapsing wall.

Once through the wall, turn left beside it, descending easily, and finally bear right to join the outward route at NM473533. Now simply retrace your steps back to the road.

The summit of 'S Airde Beinn

The loch is not very large, but it is sheltered, and, like all Mull lochs, has an indigenous stock of brown trout.

WALK 1.9

Calgary Bay and Caliach Point

Start/Finish	Calgary Bay car park (NM374513)
Distance	11.5km (7 miles)
Total ascent	405m (1330ft)
Terrain	Mainly untracked walking on raised beaches and across rough pasture; concludes with minor road walking
Map	OS Explorer 374 Isle of Mull North and Tobermory

Caliach Point is the north-westerly tip of Mull, and the trig pillar there is an outstanding viewpoint. The walk from Calgary Bay, one of Mull's finest white-sand beaches, is not without its splendours, but requires good navigational skills, as all the western part of this walk is virtually trackless (although paths do come and go somewhat optimistically), leaving you to navigate freely around rocky outcrops, inlets from the sea, and walls, none of which is unduly difficult. Overall, the walking is dry underfoot, with a couple of exceptions (that can be avoided); certainly the scenery is excellent both close by and of the distant islands, and especially so on clear days when the Outer Hebrides are visible.

Leave Calgary Bay by walking along the track from the car park, through a gate and then easily along to the old jetty, directly below a spectacular dyke. This dyke was formed when molten rock was forced upwards through cracks in harder rocks, all of which have now been worn away, leaving the intrusion as the last rock standing. The jetty itself was used to ferry cattle and sheep out to Treshnish Islands for summer pasturage.

Just before reaching the jetty, turn inland, and walk up to a gate. Higher up, pass through another gate on the left to walk beside a fence. At the top, you begin a lovely

walk along a raised beach, which gives generally easy walking, as the route presses on to round **Cnoc Udmail** and begins its journey northwards. ▶

Once you start heading northwards, the route finding is less certain, but in a way much more pleasurable – the author has passed this way on a number of occasions, and has yet to follow his earlier footsteps, although a sustained and continuous path is slowly appearing. But the lack of clear direction is no great hardship – quite the opposite on a good day. It is such a joy to walk along this remote coastline with numerous cameos of rugged sea cliffs and distant islands. The important thing is to stay well clear of the actual coastline, as much as possible, and to take care if sheep are in the vicinity. There is a tendency, too, to wander too far inland, but a little patience

There is evidence of previous settlement along this coastline, with the remains of buildings, walls, cultivation terraces and numerous paths.

and ingenuity will eventually bring you to a very substantial and well-built wall that runs in a south-westerly direction from Port na Caillich.

CALGARY BAY

Calgary is Mull's most beautiful beach, a golden strand ringed by steep wooded slopes with views across to Coll and Tiree. Canadians may be interested to note that the large city in Alberta was named after this former township. Many emigrants were forcibly shipped to Canada from here during the Clearances.

Calgary Bay is said to be a favourite haunt of Mer-folk, and island girls often married mermen, as their brothers might take to a mermaid. Such marriages, by all accounts, were invariably happy. Mer-folk who became mortal, however, had to shed their tails, and one was found by a young boy from Calgary Bay. He tried it on, tying it with a belt of seaweed, and went into the sea, but quickly realised that there was more to swimming than using a borrowed tail. As he was sinking for the third time, he felt hands bearing him up, and found himself in the arms of a mermaid, who carried him safely back to shore before slipping away, taking the cast-off tail with her.

The path through the machair at Calgary Bay

The wall below Caliach Point (sometimes Cailleach) was built by **Colonel MacKenzie**, who was renowned for breeding Arab horses and highland ponies. It was beyond the wall that he used to keep his stallions, to separate them from his other horses and ponies. The whole area of Caliach up to Sunipol was used in this way, and covered the site of a cleared village. The men who built the wall were paid in meal.

The coastline above Port na Cailich, Caliach Point

If you propose to visit the trig pillar on Caliach Point, then as you reach the wall, there are two possibilities, depending on where you intercept it. The first is to go south-west (left) to its very end (do not attempt to clamber over it), where you can, with care, step over a low fence, turn immediately right through a gate, and then bear left across splendid short turf, following a grassy path that will guide you in the general direction of Caliach Point, but not all the way to the summit. The second option

63

is to bear north-east (right) alongside the wall, crossing an intermediate fence, and continuing on to reach two gates on the left. Pass through the first of these, and take a grassy, on-going path towards a line of low crags ahead, through and around which there are many easy ways, and beyond, a gentle stroll to the trig pillar.

From the trig, the key is to return to that gate, and from there, walk across to reach a broad track that leads out to the end of the surfaced road at **Caliach Farm**.

Road walking now remains, following a narrow lane across the Mornish farmlands to reach the main Calgary road, and there turning right to complete the walk. If you enjoy free-range coastal walking, then it is possible to leave the road just beyond Caliach Farm, and plot your own route across mainly short turf, before turning inland to rejoin the road at **Sunipol**.

It is quite a long walk back to **Calgary** on the road, but it crosses a superb landscape, and the road walking is no hardship.

Although not part of this walk, it is a worthwhile diversion to visit **Port Langamull** and the superb golden sands of Bàgh Chrossapol. The key to this remote and very isolated beach is the forest track that leaves the road at NM395519, and leads to the farmstead at Langamull, from where a track runs onwards to the coast.

WALK 1.10

Treshnish

Start/Finish	Old quarry on B8073 (NM361485)
Distance	10.5km (6½ miles)
Total ascent	295m (965ft)
Terrain	Access tracks; raised beach; moorland; some road walking
Map	OS Explorer 374 Isle of Mull North and Tobermory

A splendid walk to reach the coastline, where the walk eases on along a lovely raised beach offering superb seaward views that embrace the islands of Coll and Tiree and on some days the Outer Hebrides. The walk visits two isolated settlements cleared in the 19th century, before concluding with a delightful romp across heather moorland. This is one of the finest walks on Mull.

Leave the quarry parking area and turn right, walking as far as a turning on the left for Treshnish and Haunn holiday cottages. Follow the signed path through **Treshnish Farm**, and, later, as you approach the **Haunn** cottages, leave the track for a branching path on the right, crossing rough pasture to a gate. Beyond, continue across coastal headlands to another gate, after which you make a descent of a terraced path, and come down to reach a raised beach.

To the north at this point, a low hill, Cnoc an t-Sléibhe, shelters a stretch of raised beach known as **Coir' a' Bhrochain**, which roughly translates as 'porridge cauldron'. Here, it is said, on the day of the Big Porridge, before Easter, the islanders would make a huge pot of porridge and throw it over the cliff in honour of Mana, God of the Sea, in the hope that this would bring rewards of seaweed that they used for fertiliser.

There is the suggestion of a ruined dun on one of the small headlands, all of which are well worth exploring.

Returning to the raised beach, the scenery is already superb, with low coastal cliffs, stacks and natural arches on the seaward wide, and higher crags towering on the landward. The raised beach, too, is splendid, and provides easy going on springy turf. ◄ All around, as the year progresses, flowers come and go, bringing a brightness to the scene, and imbuing it with a fine sense of peace and tranquillity. But, whatever the time of year, whatever the weather, this is a most agreeable place to be.

The Dùn at Port Haunn, Treshnish

Continue to follow the path across the raised beach, and eventually, with Ben More coming into view in the far distance, you reach a waterfall in a narrow and steep

gully (NM351461). Cross the burn, and press on a little further until you approach the lower, wooded slopes of **Beinn Reudale**, just before which you encounter another, less steep gully on the left. The way now leads up this, following a clear path that zigzags easily up what little height there is, placing you on a moorland path at the top that leads through bracken across to the ruins of **Crackaig**.

CRACKAIG AND GLAC GUGAIRIDH

The fate of Crackaig, and nearby Glac Gugairidh, epitomises the clearance of these lands, an unyielding landscape of rock and bitter moor, roofless homes among the stones and still discernible folds in the landscape that once nourished meagre crops for those that lived here. Two hundred people are said to have been cleared from here in the 19th century, except for one man, reluctant to face the ignominy of a trek across Mull to a transit camp in Tobermory and who-knows-what after that as evicted crofters were cast to the sea in ships on a journey many would not survive. He chose to hang himself, from the bent and laboured ash tree you find at Crackaig, as he saw the future and his township withering away to a shabby and sorry end. Some, as Jim Crumley points out in The Heart of Mull, say that these settlements were 'not cleared as such, but gave up the ghost themselves…in an era which reviled their place in the landscape, and lifted no hand to assist them because it did not want them to stay. They were cleared out all right, as surely as if they had been burned out.'

At the time of the evictions, the proprietor is shown as Captain George MacKay, with both villages being finally cleared in 1867.

Climb beyond Crackaig to Glac Gugairidh (although Jim Crumley suggests that these names are in each other's place, and should be the other way round). Here more ruins await, solid, honest buildings still standing long after their makers, and their defilers, have passed on. They will still be here, 200 years from now; silent testimony to a sorry period in Scottish history.

Beyond Glac Gugairidh, a path continues, rising gently onto heather moorland before bringing into view the rooftop of an isolated croft, **Larrach Mhòr**, the former schoolhouse. Pass through a gate, and then continue on a waymarked, grassy path that leads round to intercept an access track. Here, turn right and walk out to meet the main road. Now turn left and simply follow the road back to the starting point.

WALK 1.11

Beinn na Drise and Beinn Bhuidhe

Start/Finish	Eas Fors car park (NM445423)
Distance	10km (6¼ miles)
Total ascent	530m (1740ft)
Terrain	Heather and bracken heath, wet in places; a little road walking
Map	OS Explorer 374 Isle of Mull North and Tobermory

Meaning 'hill of the brambles' (although few will be found these days), Beinn na Drise is a hill for the Marilyn seekers, but it is one that gives a splendid view across Loch na Keal to Ben More and its neighbours. The ascent is not unduly difficult, although paths are uncertain once you get above the Laggan Burn, and this is very much free-range country.

The walk begins at the car park for the Eas Fors waterfall, which is worthy of a post-walk visit, since you will be following its feeder burns on the way down. Start by walking in a south-easterly direction along the road for about 1km (half a mile), but then leave it (NM452418) at a track on the left that leads up to two cottages. Continue onto the moorland beyond to zigzag up the hill slope until you reach the old village of **Bruach Mhòr**.

Walk below the village to gain the Laggan Burn, and then simply follow the burn upwards. As the burn dwindles to little or nothing, bear east on grass onto **Beinn na Drise**, coping with a few false summits before finally reaching the trig pillar and shelter on the summit.

As with so many of the minor Mull summits, the view is disproportionately outstanding, and takes in Ben More and the summits that flank it, as well as the islands of Ulva, Gometra and Treshnish; indeed you can see all the way north to Quinish, and northeast to Loch Frisa.

For a simple outing, just retrace your steps. But otherwise, set off in a north-westerly direction, descending easily through a series of those lava lips that are so typical of the Mull landscape to gain the minor bump of Tom na Sealga (easily missed), and then onwards to **Beinn Bhuidhe**. ▶

This is a lovely upland walk across grass and heather moorland.

From Beinn Bhuidhe, your next objective is the small loch, **Caol-Lochan**, a tiny loch sheltering in a hollow. Just beyond the loch you encounter Allt Mòr, which lower down becomes **Allt an Eas Fors**. Your way down runs parallel to this watercourse, across rough ground. Keep a safe distance from the burn, which presents a few tricky moments on rock if you follow it too closely.

A couple of upper falls announce the imminent end of the walk, as you drop over broad lava steps and down to the road.

Eas Fors waterfall, if you want to visit it, lies across the road.

Beinn na Drise seen from the island of Ulva

WALK 1.12
Loch Frisa

Loch Frisa is the largest loch on Mull and its circuit is a long one and, in parts, rugged. If you'd rather get a flavour for Loch Frisa for a little less energy, then the linear alternative (Walk 1.13) will do just nicely. This is a restful landscape, out of sight of the sea, and with little evidence of the volcanic and Ice Age activities that have shaped the island. Both walks start from the Loch Frisa car park at the northern end of the loch, and share the eastern, open side of the valley, but travelling in opposite directions.

Circuit of Loch Frisa

Start/Finish	Loch Frisa car park (NM463522)
Distance	21km (13 miles)
Total ascent	520m (1705ft)
Terrain	Forest trails; farmland; moorland.
Map	OS Explorer 374 Isle of Mull North and Tobermory

This circuit is a significant undertaking but the anticlockwise nature of this circuit puts all the hard work into the first half, and leaves you a broad and easy forest trail along which to conclude the walk.

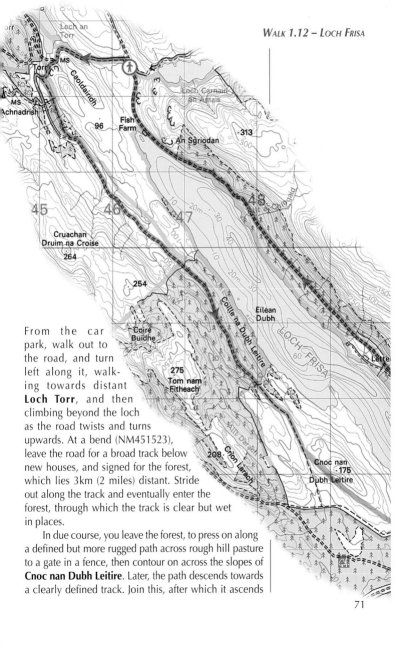

From the car park, walk out to the road, and turn left along it, walking towards distant **Loch Torr**, and then climbing beyond the loch as the road twists and turns upwards. At a bend (NM451523), leave the road for a broad track below new houses, and signed for the forest, which lies 3km (2 miles) distant. Stride out along the track and eventually enter the forest, through which the track is clear but wet in places.

In due course, you leave the forest, to press on along a defined but more rugged path across rough hill pasture to a gate in a fence, then contour on across the slopes of **Cnoc nan Dubh Leitire**. Later, the path descends towards a clearly defined track. Join this, after which it ascends gently and passes a group of **standing stones**, about which little is known.

Heading south-east you make for a clear track leading to **Tenga Farm**, where you pass through gates and turn left up a track before reaching the farmhouse. After Tenga you climb a little and then descend to another gate beyond which a footbridge spanning the **Ledmore River** comes into view. Electricity pylons guide you to the bridge, which replaces stepping stones of old.

Cross the footbridge, and walk up the ensuing fields to reach a broad forest trail. Now simply turn left along this, and follow it all the way back to the start, keeping to the higher track when it divides as you approach **Lettermore Farm**.

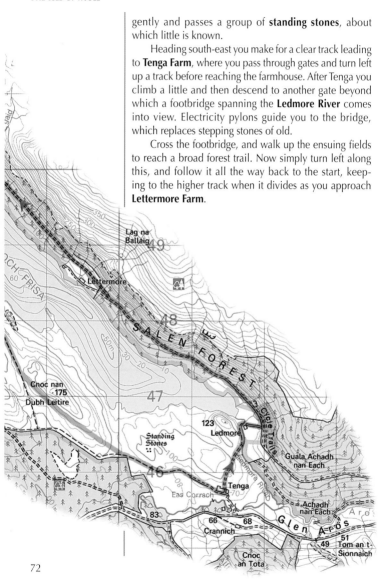

Loch Frisa linear walk

Loch Frisa

Start	Loch Frisa car park (NM463522)
Finish	Salen road car park (NM554458)
Distance	12.5km (6 miles)
Total ascent	280m (920ft)
Total descent	305m (1000ft)
Terrain	Wide forest trail throughout
Map	OS Explorer 374 Isle of Mull North and Tobermory

This linear walk is as easy as can be, and provides a lovely leisurely stroll above Loch Frisa, mostly out in the open and only succumbing to the cloistered green walls of forest towards the end. It is possible to undertake this walk using public transport, as the bus service from Tobermory to Dervaig and Calgary can drop you off at the start, while the Craignure to Tobermory bus can collect you at the other end. Otherwise, the transport logistics will need resolving.

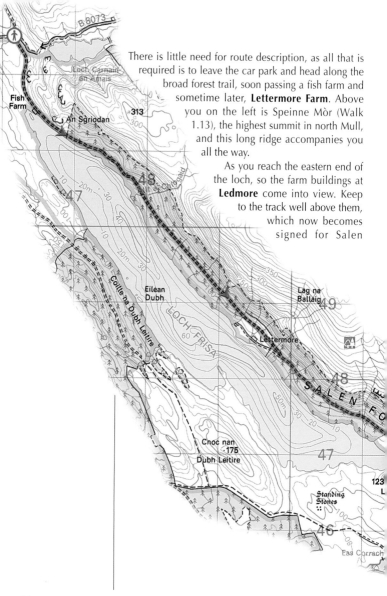

There is little need for route description, as all that is required is to leave the car park and head along the broad forest trail, soon passing a fish farm and sometime later, **Lettermore Farm**. Above you on the left is Speinne Mòr (Walk 1.13), the highest summit in north Mull, and this long ridge accompanies you all the way.

As you reach the eastern end of the loch, so the farm buildings at **Ledmore** come into view. Keep to the track well above them, which now becomes signed for Salen

road, and leads you onward through the depths of **Salen Forest** to reach the road below the minor hill of Tùr Mòr, and the end of the walk.

Loch Frisa and Lettermore farm

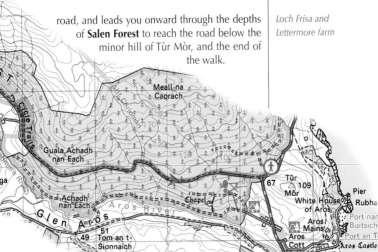

WALK 1.13

Speinne Mòr

Start/Finish	Mishnish lochs (NM465524) or Loch Frisa car park (NM463522)
Distance	11.5km (7 miles)
Total ascent	540m (1770ft)
Terrain	Heather and bracken heath, wet in places; steep descent through bracken-covered cleared forest; forest trail; a little road walking
Map	OS Explorer 374 Isle of Mull North and Tobermory

Speinne Mòr is the highest hill in the northern part of Mull, and, as might be expected, commands an excellent panorama of rippling hills far and near. The ascent is perfectly straightforward, and even the described descent to the Loch Frisa forest trail, while requiring care in the placement of feet and choice of line, is not unduly difficult.

There are two possible starting points: one is a small roadside quarry area at the western end of the Mishnish Lochs, just past Loch Carnain an Amais; the other the larger Loch Frisa car park, a little further west, downhill. Which you choose depends on whether the uphill road walking between the two is preferred at the start of the walk, or at the end.

From the quarry at the higher of the two starting points, pass through a gate nearby to gain a path through bracken that begins the ascent onto the west ridge of Speinne Mòr. ◀

There is a continuous path from here almost all the way to the summit of the hill. It traverses slightly wet ground, but nowhere presents undue difficulties.

The path rises first onto Sròn na Beinne Creagaich, and then by a succession of ledges into a section of exposed peat and underlying rock. Beyond this the path continues along a peat edge, and a little further on you pick up the

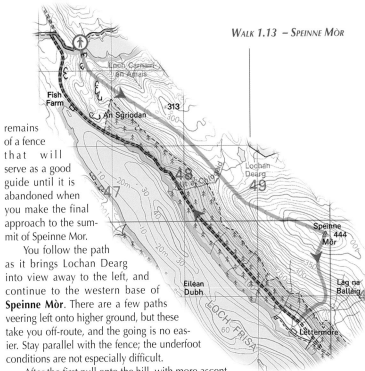

remains
of a fence
that will
serve as a good
guide until it is
abandoned when
you make the final
approach to the sum-
mit of Speinne Mor.

You follow the path
as it brings Lochan Dearg
into view away to the left, and
continue to the western base of
Speinne Mòr. There are a few paths
veering left onto higher ground, but these
take you off-route, and the going is no easier. Stay parallel with the fence; the underfoot
conditions are not especially difficult.

After the first pull onto the hill, with more ascent
still to come, you gradually leave the fenceline, and bear
left up easy, grassy slopes to the summit.

The top of the mountain is marked by a trig pillar
within a circular shelter, now infilling with bracken; a
nearby knobble of rock appears to have the same height,
both measured by GPS at 448m, some 4m higher than
the map suggests.

There are two possible ways back to the start. One
is simply to retrace your steps, giving a round trip of
8.75km (5½ miles), and 395m (1295ft) of height gain.
The other involves a steep descent to the forest trail
above Lettermore Farm. Between the top of the steep
descent and the forest trail there is a good stretch of difficult going on which walking poles would help, at least
until you reach the bracken, when they will be more of
a hindrance. The line is just west of south, targeting the

Upland moorland,
Speinne Mòr

A little studying of
the landscape before
committing yourself
to the line of descent
will minimise such
difficulties as
there are.

Allt Lag na Ballaig, although you do not want to get too close to the waterfall, which lower down dashes over a rock sill.

Although not shown on the map, there is a wide gap in the Salen Forest directly above **Lettermore Farm**, and you should head for this, taking such line as you feel comfortable with. By aiming towards the **Allt Lag na Ballaig** you find a more or less clear way down; too far to the west, and you enter an area that has been cleared of trees, but with the root balls and fallen branches concealed among bracken and heather, making the going awkward, very uncomfortable and potentially ankle-twisting. ◄ The main thing is to take it easy and be ready to change tack if the going gets too rough.

When you finally reach the forest trail simply turn right and follow it out above **Loch Frisa** until you pass the **fish farm** buildings, and then reach the road. A short uphill stretch will take you back to the higher starting point.

WALK 1.14

Salen and Cnoc na Sróine Hill Fort

Start/Finish	Salen (NM571432); limited parking near bus stop
Distance	6.25km (4 miles)
Total ascent	190m (625ft)
Terrain	Managed farmland; heathery moorland; birch woodland; muddy in places
Map	OS Explorer 374 Isle of Mull North and Tobermory

This walk exemplifies the walking on Mull, at once demanding yet rewarding, difficult underfoot at times, but at others a delight to follow. Overall it is neither too challenging nor, in spite of its brevity, too easy, but after rain you must expect some very squelchy stretches – par for many courses on Mull. The hill fort along the walk is a marvellous viewpoint; the moorland acres, and the birch woodlands that are a feature of the later stages, resound to birdsong. Walk 1.15 describes a one-way walk from Salen to Killiechronan, across the neck of Mull; taken in the reverse direction, starting and finishing at Killiechronan, the two walks can be combined into one long and satisfying walk of 10.5km (6½ miles).

Set off along the road in the direction of Tobermory, taking care against approaching traffic. Leave the road at a gate on the left (NM569435) onto a rising footpath for **Glenaros Farm**. The path initially passes through broadleaved woodland, and as you press on towards the farm, so Aros Castle comes into view on its headland.

At a double gate you reach the edge of a large pasture, and continue forward alongside a fence, soon bringing Glenaros Farm into view. As you approach the farm, pass through a metal gate and go half-left to another

AROS CASTLE

Aros Castle, built in the 13th or 14th century by the MacDougalls, is one of Mull's largest medieval castles, and second in importance to Ardtornish across the Sound of Mull as a stronghold of the Lords of the Isles.

The Lords of the Isles were actually a syndicate of clans under Macdonald of Islay, and were a constant source of trouble for the Scottish Parliament, not least because one of them, Donald Bane, was brother to King Malcolm III, and therefore had a stronger claim to the Scottish throne than had the rather better known Robert the Bruce.

gate, and then cross to the end of a surfaced lane, at **Kate's Cottage**.

Cross the lane, and, through another gate, bear left onto a broad track that runs parallel with a wall. When the wall changes direction, keep forward, moving out onto moorland slopes. Quite soon the hill of Cnoc na Sróine comes into view. Ford the Allt a' Chaisteil and press on towards the hill, and, as you draw level with it, take a path branching left up to its summit.

Cnoc na Sróine is an ancient hill fort of which there are a few remaining wall sections and what look like small rooms. A large cairn marks the highest point, from which there is a fine view across the Sound of Mull to Morvern, and north-west to Loch Frisa.

Cross the top of the hill and take a path going down on the other side to rejoin the main path. This now presses on across the moor, and is clear throughout, eventually winding down through scatterings of silver birch, rhododendron, goat willow, self-seeded spruce and widespread bog myrtle.

Eventually the path comes down to intercept another path, one that crosses the island and links Salen with Killiechronan (see Walk 1.15). Here, turn left and pursue the path, with quite a few minor diversions to avoid the worst of the boggy sections. ▸

There are a few spreads of silver birch, and where these occur, so, too, do the worst conditions underfoot.

As you emerge from the birch woodland, south of the minor hill **Bràigh a' Choire Mhòir**, the immediate way forward is not obvious, being obstructed by a burn. Other walkers have taken a line to the left here, but you then need to swing back to the right to locate the on-going track, which is clear enough once you find it.

The path wanders on easily, and then has another fling with birch woodland, through which the path threads a way back towards **Salen**, reaching the village near the former church, now a private residence. Turn right to complete the walk.

Cnoc na Sróine hill fort

WALK 1.15
Mull Coast-to-Coast: Salen to Killiechronan

Start/Finish	Salen (NM571432); limited parking near bus stop
Distance	4km (2½ miles) – one way
Total ascent	110m (360ft)
Terrain	Heathery moorland; birch woodland; muddy in places
Map	OS Explorer 374 Isle of Mull North and Tobermory

Although linear in design, this walk across the narrowest part of Mull can easily be retraced to give an out-and-back walk. It is best savoured following a long period of dry weather, as some sections of the path are frequently waterlogged. Starting from Salen has the advantage of fine forward views of Loch na Keal, above which rise Ben More, Beinn Fhada and Beinn nan Gabhar. Alternatively, you can combine this walk with Walk 1.14, starting and finishing at Killiechronan (NM540412), to take in the Cnoc na Sróine hill fort and give a longer walk of 10.5km (6½ miles).

Leave Salen by heading towards Tobermory, but immediately on passing the last building on the left, the former church, turn left up a track beside it, but at the rear of the building, leave the track for a narrow path rising into birch woodland. Follow the path, steadily upwards, as it teases a way through the woodland, wet in places, but eventually breaking free as it approaches the minor hill, **Bràigh a' Choire Mhòir**.

Press on below this hill, and the path will guide you down towards more birch woodland with a difficult entry point that requires a little dancing about to evade the wettest ground. But then a clear path runs through the woodland, which is not extensive, and soon reaches open ground again.

The path re-enters a wooded area, this time the more substantial acreage of forestry plantations. A squelchy start leads to a deer gate and an enclosed path. to another gate. The next few minutes will be found trying as you push on through the woodland, following a clear path, but one that is decidedly wet. Eventually, all this mess –

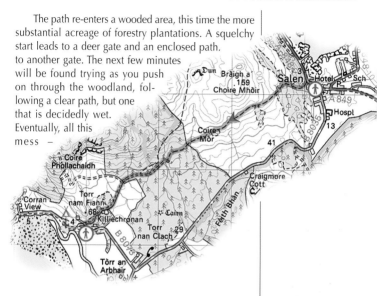

which, to be fair, is only an issue after prolonged rain – is left behind as you reach a T-junction, intersecting with a more conventional forest trail. Turn right here, and follow the trail through stands of spruce, larch and birch.

The woodland trail, bound for Killiechronan

Gradually the trees fall back, and at another deer gate you finally leave the trees behind altogether. Go forward to another broad trail, bearing left, with lovely forward views towards Loch na Keal. As you approach **Killiechronan** you reach another track junction, and should turn left here down to the road.

Without someone to pick you up at Killiechronan, you have a choice of either retracing your steps, or walking along the minor road towards Gruline, before turning left back to **Salen**. ◄

There is a bus stop at the Salen road, but buses are infrequent.

WALK 1.16
Glen Aros

Start/Finish	Glen Aros car park (NM549454)
Distance	8.8km (5½ miles)
Total ascent	145m (475ft)
Terrain	Forest trails; some road walking
Map	OS Explorer 374 Isle of Mull North and Tobermory

Loch Frisa is the largest loch on Mull, and this walk from the Salen–Tobermory road takes you easily to the edge of it, temptation possibly for tackling something a little longer, like a complete circuit of the loch (Walk 1.12). This gentle circuit of Glen Aros should tax no-one, most of it being spent trekking through mature plantation, which stands far enough back from the forest trail to eliminate any sense of claustrophobia and to allow views of the surrounding countryside. The entire experience is most restful and agreeable, whatever the weather.

The word 'aros' has Scandinavian roots, meaning an estuary.

The starting point lies at the end of a rough track, past the Forest of Lorne District Offices near Aros. ◄ From the parking area, carry on in the same direction soon to enter Salen Forest. Although the trees are mature, they are

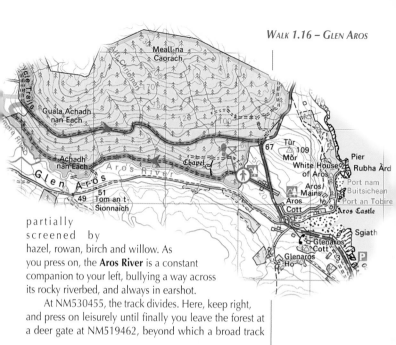

partially
screened by
hazel, rowan, birch and willow. As
you press on, the **Aros River** is a constant
companion to your left, bullying a way across
its rocky riverbed, and always in earshot.

At NM530455, the track divides. Here, keep right,
and press on leisurely until finally you leave the forest at
a deer gate at NM519462, beyond which a broad track

Loch Frisa and Ledmore farm

85

guides you on across rough pasture, now with the southern edge of Loch Frisa and Ledmore Farm in view.

The track leads up to another deer gate giving on to a higher forest track at a T-junction. Now simply turn right and follow the trail easily for some distance until finally you emerge on the Salen road just below the low hill of **Tùr Mòr**. All that remains is to walk, right, down the single-track road, taking care against approaching traffic, a distance of 650m, with a verge on the left for most of the way.

Anyone wanting to briefly visit **Tùr Mòr** will find it to be a fine viewpoint, looking down to the Sound of Mull and the vicinity of Aros Castle. A gate at the road bend, just after rejoining it, gives access to an easy grassy stroll up to the trig pillar that marks the summit. This diversion will add nominally to the distance and height gain.

Return to the road, and at the entrance to the **Forestry District Office**, leave it and walk down the track back to the starting point.

2 CENTRAL MULL

The final pull onto Mainnir nam Fiadh (Walk 2.14)

INTRODUCTION

The central section of Mull, defined in the north by the narrowing between Salen and Killiechronan, and in the south by the A849 as it courses through the Great Glen to Loch Scridain, is by far the most mountainous and a distinct contrast to the lava flows on north Mull. Here, if you know what you're looking at, it is obvious that the landscape is fashioned by massive volcanic upheavals, not least in the huge caldera, or volcanic crater, that centres on Loch Ba.

With the exception of Beinn Talaidh and Dùn da Ghaoithe in the east, and, of course, Ben More, the hills of Central Mull are rarely visited, and offer the walker days of solitude and fine walking. Ben More dominates, rising to 966m (3170ft), but there are numerous peaks over 600m worthy of the walker's attention.

Roughly central to this group of hills is Loch Ba, a magnificent sheet of water surrounded by a ring of hills fashioned when a dome of magma collapsed like a badly made soufflé, leaving only the edges standing proud above the land. Linking the north part of this group, defined by Loch na Keal, with Glen More is the sort of exercise that will appeal to walkers who are competent in extreme wilderness situations, far from outside help. But lesser mortals are not excluded from this domain, with gentle walks

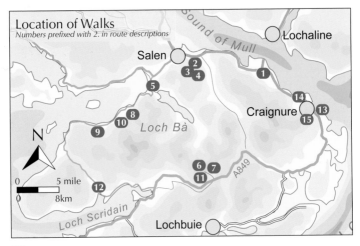

Location of Walks
Numbers prefixed with 2. in route descriptions

Sunset, Glen Forsa

to Loch Ba itself and onward through Glen Clachaig, a splendid through route, once used by drovers and virtually unsuspected to all but the most discerning readers of maps.

The extreme western edge of this group is known as Ardmeanach, and it might be argued, fancifully, that 'hard' and 'mean' in its name are fitting descriptions. This is unadulterated wilderness, where the only walk of any wisdom skims along the shores of Loch Scridain to the ancient Fossil Tree at the northern end of Camas an Fhèidh.

But what makes the central hills of Mull so appealing is the contrast. They offer easy glen walks of unimaginable beauty set against demanding mountain ascents and excellent long days in the hills. That the sea and its myriad islands near and far are almost always in view is just an added bonus.

WALK 2.1
Garmony Point and Fishnish

Start/Finish	Garmony Point (NM677402)
Distance	9.6km (6 miles)
Total ascent	135m (443ft)
Terrain	Coastal heath; forest trails
Map	OS Explorer 375 Isle of Mull East: Craignure

First impressions of the Fishnish peninsula are influenced by the mantle of pine that is the Cnocan Rainich plantation; it seems to be just trees, trees and more trees. Yet this used to be a well-populated area, with four villages. The remains of these and their associated croft lands are dotted about most of the ground covered in this walk, though the ruins are not easily spotted.

Although the walk can be shortened by starting and finishing at the Fishnish car park, there is a better introduction that sets off from Garmony Point on the northern edge of Scallastle Bay, looking across the Sound of Mull to Ardtornish Point, the basaltic escarpments of Morvern and the forests of Fiunary.

From the car park at Garmony Point take to the grassy path signed for Fishnish (and waymarked with red-banded poles), which starts through bracken and quickly leads to a footbridge spanning the Allt Achadh na Mòine. Close by is the site of Dùn Earba, of which nothing is instantly evident.

Once across the bridge, follow a lovely green path past ranks of burn-side alder, then rough coastal grasses, and rafts of heather and bog myrtle. Finally the path reaches the rocky shoreline, which it now parallels for a while before moving away to connect with a broad forest trail that gradually works a way gently upwards towards **Fishnish ferry**.

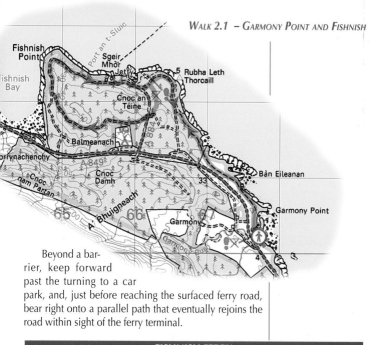

Beyond a bar-
rier, keep forward
past the turning to a car
park, and, just before reaching the surfaced ferry road,
bear right onto a parallel path that eventually rejoins the
road within sight of the ferry terminal.

FISHNISH FERRY

The ferry at Fishnish runs across the Sound of Mull to Lochaline; in years
gone by it was from here that cattle were loaded onto boats and shipped
across the Sound and north to Loch Sunart to meet up with the cattle droves
from Ardnamurchan, and then on to the trysts at Falkirk. The main cattle-
crossing point for Mull, however, was Grass Point, further to the south, from
where the cattle went to Kerrera. The Fishnish–Lochaline crossing favoured
the drovers from the north of Mull, Ulva and Gometra, who brought their
beasts to the once-important cattle market at Salen. For them, the crossing
to Morvern was a better option. Curiously, there is a local tradition that the
ferry was used to carry cattle in the opposite direction, from Morvern to
Mull, and then south to Grass Point.

Cross the road before reaching the ferry terminal,
and head up a broad forest trail, now waymarked with
green-banded poles. The trail climbs easily, passes a

91

Garmony Point,
Fishnish

quarried area and then reaches a deer gate. Gradually, the trail works its easy way round past **Fishnish Point**, and down alongside the Bay.

When the trail divides, bear left and continue through the heart of the plantation, eventually reaching another deer gate, beyond which you soon intercept the ferry road. Cross the road and go forward into a cleared area opposite. Turn immediately left, taking once more to a forest trail, but when this soon swings to the right, leave it on the apex of the bend in favour of a narrow path carpeted with moss and heather, which takes a very pleasant course through a fungi-laden plantation before finally emerging onto the track used earlier in the walk, close by the turning to the Fishnish car park. Turn right onto the trail, pass a barrier and retrace your steps to **Garmony Point**.

WALK 2.2
Glen Forsa

Start/Finish	Entrance to Glen Forsa (NM596426); vehicles are not allowed in the glen, but there is place and an invitation to park at Pennygown
Distance	7.5km (4½ miles)
Total ascent	30m (100ft)
Terrain	Gravel track through the glen; forest trail
Map	OS Explorer 375 Isle of Mull East: Craignure

This simple walk into Glen Forsa is meant to be just that, an agreeable, easy amble into one of the island's loveliest glens. The glen is key to ascents of adjacent mountains, Beinn Bhuidhe (Walk 2.3) and Beinn Talaidh (Walk 2.4), but is here offered as a virtually flat stroll that will fit neatly into a lazy afternoon or a summer's evening. A slight variation is introduced into the return leg, but essentially the walk is an out-and-back route.

The glen is an active working environment, with sheep and cattle farming a constant activity, and Highland or black cattle found on or near the track all the way; the River Forsa is popular with anglers, too. And so, while dogs are not prohibited, they must be on leads at all times. Anyone nervous in proximity to cattle should avoid this walk, or at least turn back if cattle are about.

The initial stage sets off from Pennygown and leads into the glen. Beinn nan Lus and Beinn Bhuidhe on the right are the first summits that catch your eye as you enter the glen. But then you notice the long ridge on the left which, as Walk 2.15 shows, extends all the way to Dùn da Ghaoithe above Craignure. Off to the right is Callachally Farm, and it was here and elsewhere in the glen that archaeological finds – urns, pottery and flint blades – show the glen to have been inhabited since Bronze Age times.

KILBEG

The first building you meet is the cottage at Kilbeg, where this book was largely researched and written. In the 1940s, it was lived in by a shepherd, Tom MacDonald, but transformed into a holiday cottage more than 20 years ago.

Kilbeg means 'small chapel', and just beyond the cottage, the ruins of a burial ground can be seen on the right just off the track. This and another further up the glen were destroyed when the glen, once home to 10 or more crofting families, was cleared. In a cruel gesture, typical of the period, a sheepfold was constructed on the burial site to discourage people from returning.

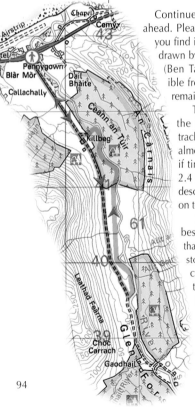

Continue past **Kilbeg** and through the gate ahead. Please ensure that you leave the gate as you find it. Now, ahead, your attention will be drawn by the shapely profile of Beinn Talaidh (Ben Tala), a distinctive summit discernible from many parts of the island. All that remains is to walk up the glen.

This walk starts to return at a gate on the left (NM608395), where the main track through the glen and the **River Forsa** almost meet. But you can go much further if time and inclination permit, and Walk 2.4 includes what little additional route description is needed for those that press on to the bothy at Tomsleibhe.

Back at the gate, turn now to walk beside the river. (Notice the small weirs that have been constructed to help the fish stocks.) Eventually, the riverside path comes to a gate at the boundary of the **Ceann an Tùir forest**. Go forward through the gate and into the forest, continuing to follow the river. This is the only stretch were the conditions underfoot are anything less than excellent, and there are a few, brief boggy patches along the way.

Finally, the path turns you back out to the glen, reaching the main track close by the cottage at Kilbeg. Turn right and walk out of the glen back to **Pennygown**.

Looking back along Glen Forsa

WALK 2.3

Beinn nan Lus and Beinn Bhuidhe

Start/Finish	Entrance to Glen Forsa (NM596426); vehicles are not allowed in the glen, but there is place and an invitation to park at Pennygown
Distance	10km (6¼ miles)
Total ascent	410m (1345ft)
Terrain	Tussocky mountain heath
Map	OS Explorer 375 Isle of Mull East: Craignure

These two low hills greet you the moment you turn in to Glen Forsa; that Beinn Bhuidhe is a Marilyn makes them irresistible. That aside, the two combine to make an excellent short walk, one that offers fine views back to Morvern on the Scottish mainland, and ahead to the summits at the ▶

95

head of the glen. You can dash in, bag the summit and dash back out again, or, as suggested here, continue the walk in a south-easterly direction, gradually descending to the main glen track (see Walk 2.2) at any one of many opportunities.

Beinn nan Lus and Beinn Bhuidhe from Glen Forsa

From the parking area walk into the glen, but please note that this is an active working environment, and cattle and sheep are often on or near the track, although they tend not to stray too far above it. Dogs must be kept on leads.

After about 1.25km (0.8 miles), you pass Kilbeg cottage, beyond which you soon reach a gate across the track. Through the gate, leave the track and take to the squelchy moorland on the right, following the line of a deer fence, which a little higher up, changes direction, as you now cross slightly better ground. You can change direction with it, and follow it until you intercept a long waterslide, more noticeable as you enter the glen than close up. Or you can cut corners a little and head straight up.

There is no need to cross the waterslide; simply finding the dry ground and working a way easily upwards will soon bring you to the trig pillar of **Beinn nan Lus**, followed by easy walking across to **Beinn Bhuidhe**, which is a little higher and marked by a large cairn. There is another Beinn Bhuidhe close by, but the two cannot be confused. In fact, there are many Beinn Bhuidhes on Mull, seven or more. The name means 'yellow (or golden) hill'.

Return the same way, or for a longer outing press on along this lovely ridge, steadily descending in a south-easterly direction. There are many places where you can drop down to the glen track at any time, although you may have to leap valiantly over a drainage ditch, and it would be wise to study the spread of bracken below, which can be tiresome to plough through.

By gradually following the fall of the ridge you will come down to regain the glen track near **Gaodhail**, and, on doing so, turn left to walk back out along the glen to **Pennygown**. Walk 2.2 gives a minor variation for this return leg.

WALK 2.4
Beinn Talaidh

Start/Finish	Entrance to Glen Forsa (NM596426); vehicles are not allowed in the glen, but there is place and an invitation to park at Pennygown
Distance	17.5km (11 miles)
Total ascent	750m (2460ft)
Terrain	Gravel track through Glen Forsa; rough moorland; upland grass and scree
Map	OS Explorer 375 Isle of Mull East: Craignure

Beinn Talaidh (pronounced Tala) has a distinctive profile: clean, sweeping, almost conical, sitting at the head of Glen Forsa with its acolyte, Beinn Bheag, tucked to one side like a dutiful servant. Arguably, after Ben More, this is Mull's most distinctive peak, and edges itself into many views. Until resurveying proved otherwise, Beinn Talaidh was always regarded as a Corbett, a mountain over 2500ft; now its revised height of 761m only converts to 2496ft, which moves it into the Donald camp, or at least it would if it were in southern Scotland. (In fact, it is classifed as a Graham!) Setting aside these niceties, Beinn Talaidh is a fine mountain to climb, especially, if as described here, it is approached by the long walk in and out of Glen Forsa.

Memorial to aircrash, Glen Forsa

The start of the walk could not be easier; it begins at the entrance to Glen Forsa, and simply marches onward, further and further into this lovely defile, passing Kilbeg cottage and the ruins of a chapel and graveyard, before pressing on towards the sheep stations at the head of the glen. In the past, there were as many as 10 or more families living in the glen, but they were evicted at the time of the Clearances.

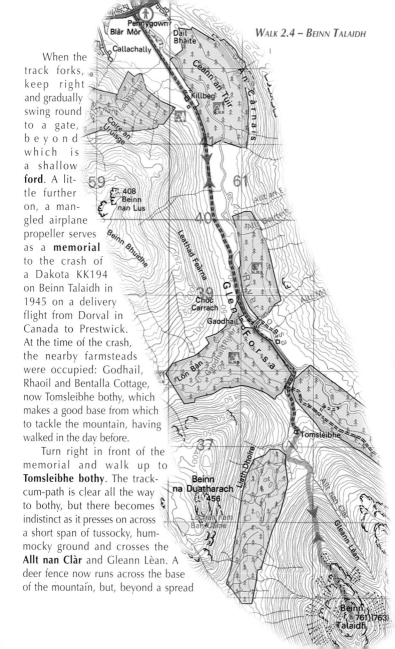

When the track forks, keep right and gradually swing round to a gate, beyond which is a shallow **ford**. A little further on, a mangled airplane propeller serves as a **memorial** to the crash of a Dakota KK194 on Beinn Talaidh in 1945 on a delivery flight from Dorval in Canada to Prestwick. At the time of the crash, the nearby farmsteads were occupied: Godhail, Rhaoil and Bentalla Cottage, now Tomsleibhe bothy, which makes a good base from which to tackle the mountain, having walked in the day before.

Turn right in front of the memorial and walk up to **Tomsleibhe bothy**. The track-cum-path is clear all the way to bothy, but there becomes indistinct as it presses on across a short span of tussocky, hummocky ground and crosses the **Allt nan Clàr** and Gleann Lèan. A deer fence now runs across the base of the mountain, but, beyond a spread of glacial moraine, there is a gate that lets you on to the mountain.

Which line you now take is a matter of choice. The ascent is steep whichever way you go, but it is a little easier to backtrack into **Gleann Lèan** to gain less marshy ground, and then to simply pull up onto the north ridge of **Beinn Talaidh**, and follow it to the summit.

The highest point is marked by a cairn, not the trig pillar. The panorama is outstanding, although views to the east and north-east, to Ben Nevis, are blocked by the bulk of Dùn da Ghaoithe.

The surest way to return is to retrace your steps, and savour the long, easy walk out down **Glen Forsa**.

Beinn Talaidh and the Tomsleibhe bothy

WALK 2.5
Loch Ba

Start/Finish	Knock (NM546388)
Distance	7.5km (4¾ miles)
Total ascent	30m (98ft)
Terrain	Broad, well-surfaced trail throughout
Map	OS Explorer 374 Isle of Mull North and Tobermory, and 375 Isle of Mull East: Craignure

This out-and-back walk could not be simpler – virtually level and on a good track throughout. Yet it is so delightful, easing along beside Loch Ba, 'loch of the cattle', in which, on a still day, when the silence is deafening, the hills to the east – Na Binneinean and Beinn na Duatharach – are mirrored perfectly. This is a good walk on which to take binoculars, as the birch woods that line part of the route are popular with siskin, goldcrest and the various members of the tit family, while merganser, sandpiper, geese and swan are often seen on the loch and around its shoreline.

There is a small parking area just at the acute road bend in Knock, and from here you turn onto a broad track into the Benmore Estate. The track enters the glen below steep hill slopes rising ultimately to Beinn Ghraig, but opposite **Benmore Lodge** reaches the edge of **Loch Ba**. Now the route keeps beside the loch, leading on in the most agreeable fashion. ▸

Along the way you twice pass through light woodland cover – all part of the **Coille na Sròine** – mainly of birch, oak, rowan, willow, alder and hazel. As you pass a small fish farm, the way up the glen becomes wider, and, at its head, the smooth-sided profile of Beinn Talaidh rises dramatically.

The loch is an exquisite stretch of water, surrounded by heather-clad hills on which deer may be spotted, and over which eagles patrol.

THE ELIXIR OF LIFE

According to legend, there was a time when the waters of Loch Ba had magical qualities, capable of restoring youth to the aged. This was in the days of the Witch of Mull, the giantess Caliach Bheur, who lived in a time so long ago that the lands on which her herds of deer roamed have long since been reclaimed by the sea. She was so tall that when she waded across the Sound of Mull, the water was barely knee deep. Stones and earth that toppled from her creel became the foundations of Mull's many islands.

Caliach Bheur grew old, like everyone else, but by immersing herself in the waters of Loch Ba early on the morning of each 100th birthday, she was restored to girlhood. But the feat had to be completed before any living creature uttered its first call of the day. Alas, as once again she teetered slowly towards the loch, she heard the sound of barking from a restless dog, and the spell was broken. Caliach Bheur died only a few strides from the water's edge.

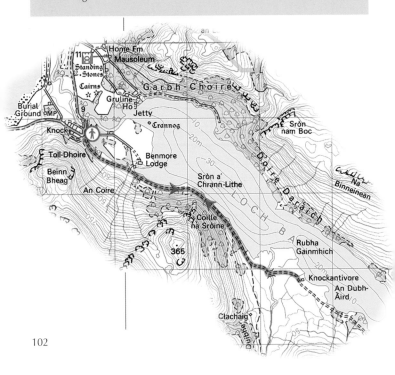

Loch Ba

At NM568371, the track forks. The track to the right leads by an old drove road through Glen Clachaig and over into Glen More. But here, you take the left branch, and soon reach the bridge spanning the **Clachaig river**. A short way further on lies the isolated building at **Knockantivore**, from where you retrace your steps to the start of the walk, although you can, if you wish, wander further on into Glen Cannel.

At the head of Glen Cannel, **Beinn Chàigidle**, is what remains of a double volcano that existed here, 50–60 million years ago, and rose to almost 2800m (9000ft). Almost five miles wide, the volcano spewed out most of the lava that formed the ancient land floor of Mull.

WALK 2.6
Glen More to Loch Ba

Start	Teanga Brideig, A849 (NM564307); limited parking along former highway, near old bridge
Finish	Knock (NM546388)
Distance	11.5km (7 miles)
Total ascent	320m (1050ft)
Total descent	350m (1150ft)
Terrain	Mountain upland; boggy paths; fords; broad trail
Map	OS Explorer 375 Isle of Mull East: Craignure

The old bridge at Teanga Brideig is an excellent starting point for this linear trek along an old drove route, across into the glacial creation that is Glen Clachaig, and out on along the shores of Loch Ba. If you follow it in this south to north direction, it will be necessary to give some thought to transport arrangements; although buses run through Glen More, none passes through Knock at the end of the walk.

The same starting point, and the same early stages of the route, is used for ascents of Ben More over A' Chioch (Walk 2.11) and of the Marilyn Corra-bheinn and neighbouring Cruachan Dearg (Walk 2.7). The route, in reverse, is one of the ancient drove roads used to move cattle across Mull, grazing as they went, in readiness for transfer from Grass Point to Kerrera, and onward to the trysts at Crieff and Falkirk.

The scenery is excellent throughout, rising within 3km (2 miles) to a mountain pass, before descending into Glen Clachaig and on to Loch Ba. The terrain is not unduly demanding, but there are a few boggy stretches along the paths, and fords, notably that of the Clachaig river, to deal with, although these are rarely in impassable conditions.

Cross the ancient bridge spanning the **Allt Teanga Brideig** and immediately turn left to a gate, beyond which the old path sets about the lower slopes of Corra-bheinn, zigzagging a little to ease the ascent. In dry or frozen conditions, the walk up to the bealach is magnificent, but there is usually enough water about to call for nimble footwork to avoid the worst clutches. The path, however, remains continuous and clear throughout.

Further up, Torr na h-Uamha seems to present an obstacle, but the path passes to its left once you cross the Allt Coir' an t-Sailein, and then it is plain sailing up to the bealach, Mam Clachaig, just east of **Creag MhicFhionlaidh**. Here you find a modest cairn, Carn Cul Righ Albainn, which translates as 'the cairn with its back to Scotland', an allusion to the legend that the pass formerly marked the boundary between the Picts and the Scots.

Ahead you step into the beautiful glacial **Glen Clachaig**, a superb, smooth-profiled defile. On the far side, the southern end of Beinn Fhada is shapely and inviting, while off to the left, the slope leads up to the cone of A' Chioch.

From Carn Cul Righ Albainn, the route turns down into Glen Clachaig, a clear

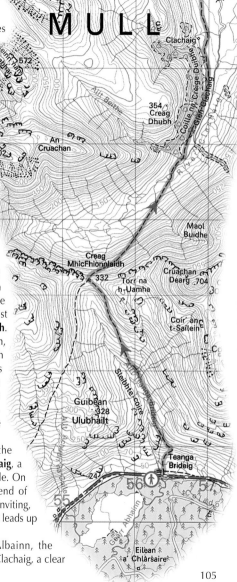

MAM CLACHAIG

This high pass is the route used by cattle drovers bringing cattle not only from Mull but from the islands of Coll and Tiree. Trade in cattle from Argyll existed from the time of Mary Queen of Scots, but it was not a task free from hazard, if the number of cases of cattle theft dealt with by the Privy Council during the 16th and 17th centuries is anything to go by. Notwithstanding, during the main droving period in the 18th and early 19th centuries, Mull continued to be one of the principal sources of droving cattle, numbering, with those from neighbouring islands, as many as 2000 head of cattle per year. The cattle were shipped from Mull at Grass Point at the mouth of Loch Don to the island of Kerrera. Even at the end of the 18th century, Oban was, as Dr Johnson described, 'only a small village if a few houses can be so described', so the cattle were taken to Kerrera, from where they swam the narrow channel to the mainland.

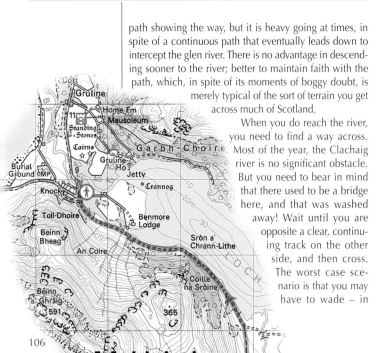

path showing the way, but it is heavy going at times, in spite of a continuous path that eventually leads down to intercept the glen river. There is no advantage in descending sooner to the river; better to maintain faith with the path, which, in spite of its moments of boggy doubt, is merely typical of the sort of terrain you get across much of Scotland.

When you do reach the river, you need to find a way across. Most of the year, the Clachaig river is no significant obstacle. But you need to bear in mind that there used to be a bridge here, and that was washed away! Wait until you are opposite a clear, continuing track on the other side, and then cross. The worst case scenario is that you may have to wade – in

Loch Ba

which case walking poles, along with dry socks and a towel, would be useful.

Once across the river, the rough, on-going track, already much better than hitherto, steadily improves as it runs out to the croft at Clachaig (not the ruin the map suggests). From here a broad track takes over, leading down to a junction just above **Loch Ba**. Turn left here, and simply follow the track out.

The contrast with what has gone before could not be greater. Here, the loch is backed by heathery hills, and the going underfoot of the easiest kind. And although the walk out is now easy, and not far, a fine sense of mountain remoteness lingers on, an away-from-it-all that bears a keen sense of volcanic Mull's origins.

Millions of years ago, long before the Ice Ages that later fashioned the smooth sides of, a huge mound of magma was forced upwards like rising dough in an oven. But when the tension could no longer be sustained, the centre of the mound collapsed, leaving behind the great ring of hills that circle the head of Loch Ba. Even in poor conditions, the scenery is marvellous; on a fine day, anglers sit out in boats, while a different type of angler, arguably more efficient – red-breasted merganser and cormorant – dive the waters. It is all very idyllic and peaceful.

With the hard work done, it is quite a joy to ramble along beside the loch, as described in Walk 2.5, the track taking you all the way out to the village of **Knock**.

WALK 2.7
Corra-bheinn and Cruachan Dearg

Start/Finish	Teanga Brideig, A849 (NM564307); limited parking along former highway, near old bridge
Distance	8.5km (5¼ miles)
Total ascent	795m (2610ft)
Terrain	Mountain upland; boggy paths; fords
Map	OS Explorer 375 Isle of Mull East: Craignure

Corra-bheinn and Cruachan Dearg are easily overlooked among the hills of Mull, other than by walkers who are tackling the Marilyns. Both summits lie north of the A849 Glen More road, and both have the same height, but the re-ascent between the two hills is less than the 150m needed for both to qualify for Marilyn status. The principal guide in these matters admits, 'It is a somewhat arbitrary decision to include one rather than the other'. Perhaps the fact that, unlike Cruachan Dearg, Corra-bheinn has a trig pillar made all the difference. But it does show what difficulties you can get into when trying to impose man-made rules on Nature.

On the assumption that most people visiting Corra-bheinn will be doing so to put a tick on a list, the following route description offers the simplest line of ascent, but makes the effort to turn the outing into a more gratifying circuit. The going is typically rough Scottish terrain, only attaining anything approaching dry walking conditions once the summits and the ridge linking them is reached – and not always then. But there is pleasure in tackling the hills for their own sake, as they are splendid vantage points and worthy of ascent on that count alone.

The key to the ascent is an old bridge on a disused section of the Glen More road at Teanga Brideig. The early stages of the walk are shared with two others: Walk 2.6, which crosses into Glen Clachaig and Loch Ba, and Walk 2.11, which heads via A' Chioch for Ben More, and is considerably more demanding.

Cross the bridge over the **Allt Teanga Brideig** and immediately turn left to a gate, beyond which the path sets about the lower slopes of Corra-bheinn, zigzagging a little to ease the ascent. The path is clear enough, but rather boggy, making dry or frozen conditions a better state, although with snow on these two summits, they become a quite different proposition.

Press on up the glen, above the Allt Teanga Brideig, as far as the point where the Allt Coir' an t-Sailein comes flowing down, roughly at NM560320. Now leave the main path, and branch in a north-easterly direction,

*Cruachan Dearg from
Carn Cul Righ Albainn*

vaguely parallel with the burn until you reach the corrie, **Coir' an t-Sailein**. The ascent is wet, and tiresome
in places, and, as soon as you feel able to do so, bear
right (south-east) towards Corra-bheinn. There is no
path, so it is simply a question of choosing a line that
best suits you. There is a ridge linking the two summits, **Màm a' Choir' Idhir**, and once you are on this,
it is a fairly simple matter to turn in one direction to
Corra-bheinn, and then return and go the other way to
reach **Cruachan Dearg**.

Alas, you need to include both summits against
the possibility that the list-makers will at some time in
the future change their minds about which summit gets
Marilyn status, or improvements in surveying techniques
shows one to be a few centimetres higher than the other,
which surely must be the case. In any event, lists aside, it
is an agreeable, albeit demanding, outing to tackle both
summits.

From Cruachan Dearg, you can simply retrace your
steps; that is the easiest option. But, by descending steeply
in a north-westerly direction, then veering to the south-
west, you will cross the shoulder of **Torr na h-Uamha**,
and arrive at the neat bealach that contains the Carn Cul
Righ Albainn, 'the cairn with its back to Scotland'.

Here, now turn southwards and follow a clear path
back down the Allt Teanga Brideig, returning eventually
to **Teanga Brideig**.

WALK 2.8
Beinn nan Gabhar and Beinn Fhada

Start/Finish	Bridge over Scarisdale River, Loch na Keal (NM517375)
Distance	9.5km (6 miles)
Total ascent	830m (2725ft)
Terrain	Rocky mountain upland; steep ascents and descents
Map	OS Explorer 375 Isle of Mull East: Craignure

This is often the place to be when neighbouring Ben More is wreathed in cloud, for these two lower mountains offer a fine alternative, albeit one that is certainly more demanding than the conventional ascent of Ben More from Dhiseig. Beinn nan Gabhar is the lower of the two main summits, while Beinn Fhada is a splendid narrow rocky ridge of considerable delight. Like all that surrounds them, these two summits are the product of the volcanic upheavals of distant times, and make excellent walking. Of course, a clear day brings excellent views of Ben More and A' Chioch as well as the undulating reaches of north Mull.

There is plenty of space to park on the foreshore near the Scarisdale bridge, allowing you to set off on a narrow path along the true right bank, crossing slightly boggy ground to a wall gap. A climb through bracken now awaits, keeping to the north of the **Scarisdale River**, which here is in a narrow and steep-sided gorge. Quite where you cross the river largely depends on its flow, but there are a few places where natural stepping stones facilitate a dry-shod crossing.

A path rounds the northern end of **Beinn nan Gabhar**, from which you can zigzag up its northern ridge, crossing scree in places and a few small rock bands before reaching a neat summit plateau. Very few walkers venture this

Beinn nan Gabhar from Loch na Keal

way, and while the mountain's name means 'hill of the goats', it is more likely to be red deer that you encounter.

From the summit the way lies down easy grassy slopes, roughly in a southerly direction, to a moderately boggy bealach below **An Cruachan**, and with the high point of Beinn Fhada off to the right. Climb up onto the ridge, and gradually move to the right (west) to romp up to a splendid summit and a superb rocky crest from which the views, notably of Ben More, are quite stunning.

Leave the top of **Beinn Fhada** in a direction a little north of

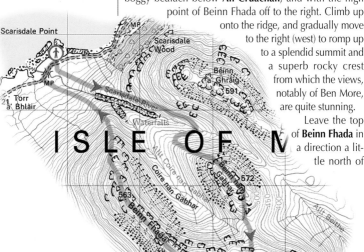

west, picking your way through a rocky band and targeting the northern end of a small lochan. Once down, set off along the splendid ridge, tackling another rock step lower down – it's slightly easier on the right – and continuing to a small, lower summit. From here the descent is easy enough to begin with, but later calls for care and attention as you pass through more rock bands. Stay as close as possible to the ridge crest, and gradually you come down to great swathes of bracken as you approach the Scarisdale River. Now the gradient eases, and the way through the bracken is neither difficult nor prolonged. A final short-lived bout of marshy ground leads back out to the road.

WALK 2.9

Ben More from Dhiseig

Start/Finish	Traigh Doire Dhubhaig, Loch na Keal (NM494395)
Distance	9km (5½ miles)
Total ascent	960m (3150ft)
Terrain	Rugged and rocky mountain upland; scree
Map	OS Explorer 375 Isle of Mull East: Craignure

If there is an easy way of climbing Ben More, Mull's highest mountain and only Munro, then this is it. But you should immediately discount the word 'easy'. Starting at sea level, you climb every inch of the way to the summit, and you will certainly know about it when you reach the top. This is a serious mountain, and much of the upper section is scree and rock. The mountain dominates many views across Mull, and for this reason should be attempted only in good visibility; the views are magnificent.

For a simple ascent of this worthy mountain, the way up from Dhiseig cannot be bettered, although there are other routes that are more classically mountainous.

From the shoreline of Loch na Keal, there is a track that leads up to **Dhiseig**. From here a clear track then crosses moorland, never far from the **Abhainn Dhiseig**, ascending all the time at a fairly easy angle, and intermittently boggy.

Eventually, however, the gradient steepens as you ease up onto the eastern spur of **Coire nam Fuaran**, and suddenly the 'big mountain' deserves its name. Higher up, the way past a rock buttress is marked by cairns, and the impression gained is that the summit lies only a short way above. But Ben More has a false summit, and it is some time until you finally come into sight of the actual summit across a well-defined path leading to a basic shelter.

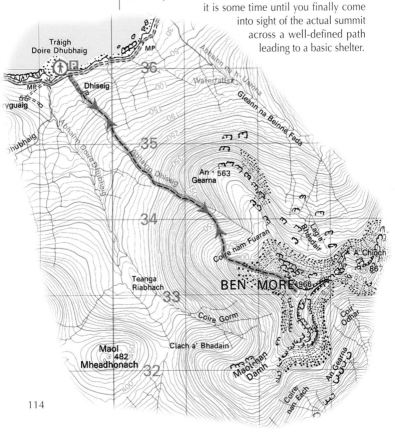

Ben More (L) and A'Chioch from Loch na Keal

Much silliness has found its way into print about how, with the building of a bridge to the Isle of Skye, **Ben More** is now the only island Munro in Scotland. Such nonsense ignores the fundamental reality that an island should be determined by its natural, not its man-made, state – and in its natural state Skye is still an island and always will be.

As might be expected, the views are magnificent and extend northwards to Ben Nevis and west, on a good day, as far as Ireland, where the Mountains of Mourne form a hazy blue ripple on the skyline. This is a quite splendid moment, and worth every last ounce of effort in getting here. ▶

There are better ways to the top of Ben More, but the route from and back to Dhiseig is hugely satisfying and popular.

115

WALK 2.10

A' Chioch and Ben More
via Gleann na Beinne Fada

Start/Finish	Shore of Loch na Keal, about 2km north-east of the Dhiseig parking area (NM507368)
Distance	12.5km (8 miles)
Total ascent	1075m (3525ft)
Terrain	Moorland tracks; rough and rocky mountain upland
Map	OS Explorer 375 Isle of Mull East: Craignure

This ascent of Ben More is arguably the finest; it is certainly quite spectacular and leads walkers through a wide glen before climbing to tackle the shapely summit of A' Chioch, then turns its attention to the main summit. The descent makes use of the conventional ascent from Dhiseig, although on a clear day strong walkers would have no problem picking a way down the heather and tussock slopes of An Gearna to rejoin the outward route. This optional finish is trackless and quite demanding, and should not be contemplated by any other than the strongest and most experienced walkers. Ben More's location, so close to the sea does, alas, mean that it often attracts cloud when all peaks around it are free. But on a good day, this ascent cannot be bettered.

Find the spot where the **Abhainn na h-Uamha** passes beneath the Loch na Keal road, and follow the river upwards through rocks to find an improving path that courts a series of mini-cascades, pools and waterfalls. Gradually, the path climbs above the river gorge, and steadily works its way up the glen, crossing numerous tributary burns along the way, and quite early on in the walk passing a fine display of **waterfalls** as you head into the upper corrie.

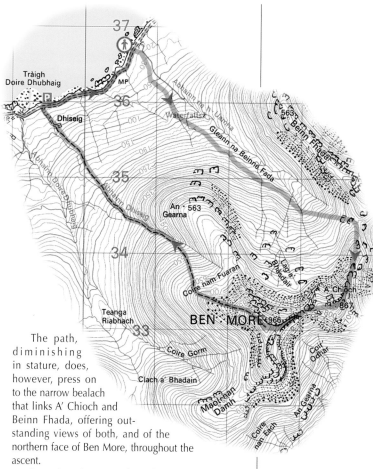

The path, diminishing in stature, does, however, press on to the narrow bealach that links A' Chioch and Beinn Fhada, offering outstanding views of both, and of the northern face of Ben More, throughout the ascent.

From the col, turn southwards and plod steadily up to the summit of shapely **A' Choich**, beyond which Ben More rises invitingly. An easy descent from A' Chioch, roughly south-westwards, leads to a superb airy walk, an ascending ridge, that rises through broken rocks and ledges to the summit of **Ben More**.

Heading for A' Chioch along the Gleann na Beinne Fada

This is really quite spectacular and exhilarating, and has been compared with the Aonach Eagach ridge in Glencoe, although there really is no comparison: the Ben More ridge, while flaky and with loose rock, is nothing like so demanding.

From the summit shelter, head across the top of the mountain to locate the numerous cairns that guide you onto the path down to Dhiseig, and complete the walk by following this down, initially through scree and a few rock bands, to gain easier ground lower down. Once at **Dhiseig**, it is a simple matter to stroll along the close-cropped lochside turf back to the start.

WALK 2.11

A' Chioch and Ben More from Glen More

Start/Finish	Teanga Brideig, A849 (NM564307); limited parking along former highway, near old bridge
Distance	12km (7½ miles)
Total ascent	1130m (3710ft)
Terrain	Mountain upland; scree; rocky ridge; boggy paths; fords
Map	OS Explorer 375 Isle of Mull East: Craignure

The ascent of Ben More from the 'Great Glen' is a route on which you are unlikely to find other walkers, unless they are following the route from Glen More to Loch Ba. There is a marked contrast between the somewhat wet terrain in Sleibhte Coire and the rocky ramparts of A' Chioch and Ben More itself. There are some issues of route finding as you work your way onto A' Chioch, suggesting that this approach is best left for a clear and settled day.

To begin with simply follow Walk 2.6 along the course of the **Allt Teanga Brideig**, passing to the west of Torr na h-Uamha to reach the cairn, Carn Cul Righ Albainn, on the bealach at the head of Clachaig glen. Ignore the path the sweeps down into Clachaig, and instead press on beyond to follow a narrow but not continuous path westwards, steeply climbing without much respite up to and through the screes of **A' Chioch**. ▶

Once on A' Chioch, you join forces with Walk 2.10, for a delightful scamper roughly westwards to the foot of a fine if loose ridge leading airily up to the summit of **Ben More**.

For the descent, you have to consider how you fared on the screes of A' Chioch. If you were happy enough, then go back this way, although you can contour south of

Initially, the screes are loose, but as you ascend they do firm up and give better footing.

A' Chioc from the summit of Ben More

the summit to intercept your line of ascent back to Carn Cul Righ Albainn.

Return via Am Binnein
Strong walkers will find pleasure in turning south from the summit of Ben More, and heading steeply downwards, swinging through to a south-westerly direction to cross lochan-dressed **Maol nan Damh** before heading south again across untracked terrain crossed by large slabs of rock to **Am Binnein**, and steeply down again across rough country finally to reach the **B8035** to Loch na Keal.

If you have to return to Teanga Brideig, simply turn left along the road – taking time out to look for otters along the shoreline of **Loch Beg** – and walk towards its junction with the Glen More A-road. Just before the T-junction, you can bear left along the old, traffic-free road for about 1km, before finally being pushed out onto the Glen More road for the final stretch to **Teanga Brideig**.

This longer circuit increases the distance to 14.5km (9 miles) – and a very demanding 14.5km at that – but adds only nominally to the height gain.

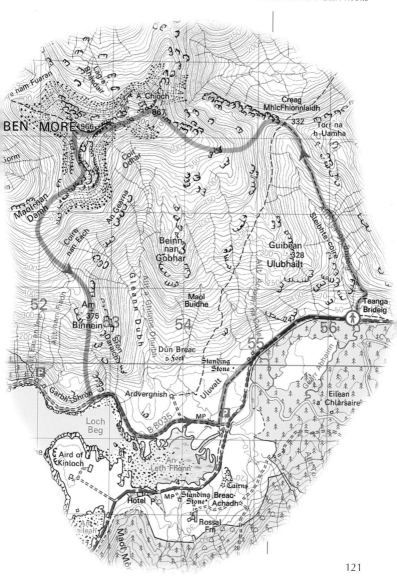

Beinn Fhada and the Carn Cul Righ Albainn

WALK 2.12
The Fossil Tree

Start/Finish	Tiroran car park (NM477276)
Distance	18km (11¼ miles)
Total ascent	730m (2395ft)
Terrain	Farm tracks; coastal path; rocky coast walking; iron ladder
Map	OS Explorer 374 Isle of Mull North and Tobermory

It is perhaps typical of Mull that its best features are not easily won. The so-called MacCulloch's Fossil Tree is a case in point. It lies at the westernmost point of the Ardmeanach peninsula and is accessible only at low tide. Fortunately, while the total distance and height gain are of the magnitude you would normally associate with the ascent of a fair-sized mountain, a wide track spurs you on for two-thirds of the distance (in both directions) and you can make good progress. It is the ruggedness that makes this walk all the more appealing, that and the likelihood that you'll have much of the walk to yourself. This is a long and arduous walk into wild and untamed scenery, where a study of the tide-table will determine whether you complete the walk or not. However, it remains a magnificent undertaking, constantly interesting and invigorating.

Key to the walk is the B8035 that runs across Ardmeanach towards Loch na Keal. From this, a narrow road branches off to Tiroran, passing behind Tiroran House, now a boutique hotel, and eventually following a rough track that leads to a National Trust car park. This is where the walk begins.

Set off along the track from the car park for Burg Farm, a comparatively straightforward exercise where speedy progress can be made. Soon after leaving the car park you pass **Scobull School**, built originally in 1898 and serving as a school until 1946. Here, where the path divides, take the right branch.

Further on, you may notice four **cairns**. These mark the spot where the coffins of the MacGillivray family were rested on the way to burial at Kilfinichen. Also here, although often hidden by bracken, are the ruins of several deserted villages, home to the estimated 300 people who lived on the Ardmeanach peninsula during the 19th century. The ridge-and-furrow pattern (lazybeds) on the landscape around the settlements are all that remain of the primitive agricultural system that supported these isolated settlements.

At Tavool, the track bears left through a gate at the edge of the wall around the garden of **Tavool House**, and then, a short way further on, **Burg Farmhouse** sits above the end of this easy track, as the way begins to become rough and uneven in places, now reduced to a path.

BURG

The small house with a sloping roof just beyond Burg farmhouse was built in the 1880s for the late Chrissie MacGillivray's parents: it is now a National Trust for Scotland bothy. Chrissie MacGillivray lived in Burg all her life, and became the local representative for the Trust at the time the property came into the Trust's care.

On the hillside behind the bothy, remnants of ancient woodland can be seen, with many trees growing in unusual shapes formed by the force of the prevailing winds. Burg was bequeathed to the National Trust for ▶

Scotland in 1932 by Mr A Campbell Blair of Dolgelly, and was one of the first properties to come into the care of the Trust. The amazing natural history and geology of this 617-hectare property are today designated a National Scenic Area and Environmentally Sensitive Area, as well as a Site of Special Scientific Interest.

Continue heading west past the bothy, passing close to the site of the Iron Age farmstead of **Dun Bhuirg**.

Within the walls of Dun Bhuirg is a memorial to **Daisy Cheape**, who drowned in August 1896. Her family owned the Tiroran and Carsaig Estates, and Daisy's unfortunate accident occurred when, aged 12, she and her brothers set out to sail round to Carsaig. It was a wild day, and the boat capsized, as a result of which young Daisy drowned.

At this point the track winds down to the beach level, following a grass-covered flat section showing traces of basic cultivation. The path rises again where the hill slope closes in on the beach, and for the next 800m is narrow. Care is required where the track crosses scree and in a few places where it has slipped down the slope. ▶

It is possible to reach the shore here, via a stream beside a steep rock rib, although this is impassable at high tide, when the sea prevents all progress. So, instead, continue a few hundred metres along the cliff top path until you reach a 20ft steel ladder attached to the cliff giving access to the bouldery beach. The approach to the ladder is steep and you need to exercise great care and caution: it is not advised for anyone suffering from vertigo or afraid of heights, but it is the way to reach the **Fossil Tree**.

Once on the beach you are left to scramble awkwardly along the shore, and pass two waterfalls that herald journey's end. The Fossil Tree lies a little further on, in a little cover beyond the second of the two waterfalls.

There are some interesting basalt formations here. Unlike those on Staffa, which are vertical, here the columns are horizontal or fan-shaped.

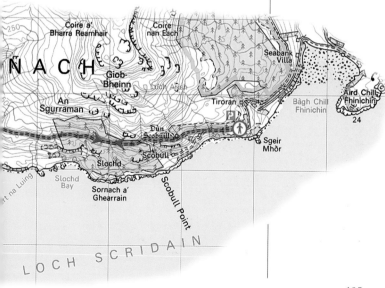

MACCULLOCH'S FOSSIL TREE

Discovered by geologist John MacCulloch in 1819, the Fossil Tree is a remarkable feature of Mull. The shape of the tree is moulded into the lava face, 12m (40ft) high and 1½m (5ft) across, and is clearly the remains of a massive tree; large enough certainly to exert a cooling effect on the flow of lava that came to engulf it, with the result that the adjacent basalt columns have been drawn inwards towards it. The tree is believed to be around 50 million years old. Sadly, much of it has been eroded by souvenir hunters, among whom it is hoped that readers of this book will not number.

All that remains is to return the way you came; the ascent of the ladder is easier than the descent. No attempt should be made to continue walking round the headland, which is in any case, accessible only at low tide, with the walking on the headland above virtually impassable. Ardmeanach means simply the 'western pasture', but 'wilderness' would be more apt.

Craignure coastline

WALK 2.13

Druim Mòr and Torosay

Start/Finish	Craignure car park (NM718370)
Distance	5.5km (3½ miles)
Total ascent	80m (260ft)
Terrain	Woodland paths; managed farmland; extensive low-level coastal walking, possibly affected by high tides
Map	OS Explorer 375 Isle of Mull East: Craignure

In spite of its brevity, this walk is hugely delightful and offers a good prospect (at least to the silent and observant walker) of seeing passing dolphins and resident otters; sea eagles, too, roam the skies, giving shape to the wind, while out to sea gannets are a common sight. The walk also provides the opportunity to visit Torosay Castle, but it is for the delights of the coastal path that it will most be remembered.

At Craignure, cross the road to a gravel shoreline path opposite the car park, and follow this until pushed back out to the roadside. Keep on in the same direction, passing the police station and the church, as far as a turning on the left at **Torosay North Lodge** (signed 'Forest Walk to Torosay Castle') (NM723366). ▶

When the track divides, branch right, climbing easily above the woodland route, to head for a **radio mast** on top of Druim Mòr. As you approach the mast enclosure, bear left through a brief, enclosed section, after which you move right to gain the grassy top of the surprisingly good viewpoint, with distant views across the Sound of Mull of Morvern, and up the length of Loch Linnhe, towards Ben Nevis. The island of Lismore is closer to hand, and in front of it the distinctive silhouette of Duart Castle.

The woodland is part of the Torosay Estate, and managed principally for conservation and landscape value.

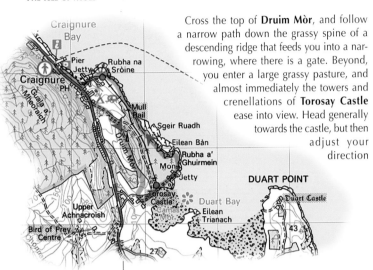

Cross the top of **Druim Mòr**, and follow a narrow path down the grassy spine of a descending ridge that feeds you into a narrowing, where there is a gate. Beyond, you enter a large grassy pasture, and almost immediately the towers and crenellations of **Torosay Castle** ease into view. Head generally towards the castle, but then adjust your direction in order to reach a narrow gate that appears below, and which gives onto a broad track, not far from the car park for the castle.

Torosay Castle is actually a fine Victorian mansion, built in 1856, in a style known as David Bryce Scottish Baronial. The castle is one of the finer examples of Bryce's work, and possibly one of a small number still lived in as a family home. Nevertheless, the castle is open to the public, and has a tea room for those in need of refreshment. The gardens include formal Italianate terraces.

Turn a matter of strides towards the castle (or go all the way if you want to pay a visit), but then swing left, down past the car park, and along a track leading to the terminus of the Torosay railway. Go past the terminus, easing into light woodland, and keep forward to pass a holiday cottage and then a boathouse opposite the jetty. Climb a few steps beyond, and take to a path through Scots pine to reach a gate, beyond which stands a large

Celtic cross memorial that you reach through a spread of montbretia and scabious. The memorial is to Murray Guthrie, who acquired Torosay Castle in 1875, and to Olive, his wife, who died on 3 July, 1945.

Go past the memorial, following a path to a gate at the corner of a spruce plantation at **Rubha a' Ghuirmein**. It is from this point onward that the likelihood of seeing dolphins and otters is greatest, but it does require, certainly in the case of the latter, a moderate and quiet approach.

The on-going path is continuous, and basically parallels the rocky shoreline, in one spot prone to immersion by seasonally high tides, but not usually unavoidably so. Even in poor weather, this coastal path is enjoyable, but it comes to an end as you round **Rubha na Sròine**; there are other paths that bear off left from the shoreline, but it is easy enough to hug the coastline, finally walking out past the Craignure village hall and the police station to reach the main road opposite the **Craignure Inn**, an 18th-century drovers' inn. Turn right to retrace your steps to the start.

Guthrie memorial, Duart Bay

WALK 2.14
Dùn da Ghaoithe

Start/Finish	Craignure car park (NM718370)
Distance	19km (12 miles)
Total ascent	915m (3000ft)
Terrain	Mountain upland (grass and rock); hard surface walking; forest
Map	OS Explorer 375 Isle of Mull East: Craignure

Dùn da Ghaoithe (pronounced doon da goo-ee), 'the hill of the two winds', is a truly splendid mountain, everything you might want a mountain to be – shapely, rugged, blessed with good views, easy on the eye and gratifyingly pleasant to ascend. It ranks as a Corbett and a Marilyn, for those who need to bag summits by category, and dominates the village of Craignure; it is, in fact, the main mountain that greets visitors arriving from Oban on the Calmac ferry.

Making a circular walk out of the ascent of Dùn da Ghaoithe is not difficult, but it involves up to 6.25km (4 miles) of road walking, plus a long ascent of a concrete and gravel service road, all of which can be punishing on your feet. Between these bits, the walking is superb, reward enough, although there are ways of reducing the hard surface walking. With an obliging partner or colleague, who can drop you off and pick you up, all the road walking can be avoided.

There are two possible ways of concluding the walk; three if you count coming back down the way you went up. All are excellent until you pass within the managed land areas. In short, where the walk is above and beyond the influence of man, the walking is excellent; once within the area where man has had an impact, the conditions are less satisfactory.

Set off from the main car park (free) in Craignure, and immediately cross the road, turning right onto a shore-line path. This soon ends, and you are left with two ways of reaching the turning at NM726394 (the first turning

on the right after the main entrance to **Torosay Castle**), where the uphill work really begins. Either walk along the road, taking care against approaching traffic – there is a short parallel path (signed 'Torosay Castle via Hedgehog Wood') that leaves the road just after the single track section starts, and spares you a little of the speeding traffic. But when this becomes surfaced and the path through Hedgehog Wood bears left, you stay on the surfaced lane and soon emerge onto the main road until you reach the turning. Alternatively, take the track that leaves the road at Torosay North Lodge (NM723366) (signed 'Forest Walk to Torosay Castle'), and follow this until it swings round towards the castle. Continue past the castle to rejoin the main road, turning left, now for only a short distance to the turning. This variant is by far the safest, and considerably more agreeable, but is a little longer than simply following the road.

Having left the main road, turn immediately right up a lane which climbs to pass a farm at **Upper Achnacroish**.
▶ Just before the farm, a gated area on the right, which formerly served the Birds of Prey Centre, is a turning point for anyone that has been able to drive you this far.

The trail around Maol na Uan

The Birds of Prey Centre that used to be here (and is still shown on maps), closed in 2009.

131

Ahead, across the on-going track, lies a gate and tall stile. Do not drive beyond this point. From here

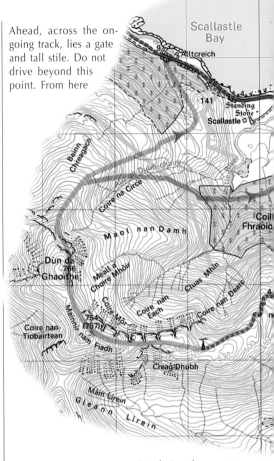

Here, the great bowl of Coire Mòr separates you from your objective to the west, shapely when viewed from this angle, but not so impressive as the cliffs of Mainnir nam Fiadh on the south side of the corrie.

on, you are on your own. But during the ascent, the views are magnificent reaching north-east along Loch Linnhe to Ben Nevis, 58km (36 miles) distant, the Mamores, the Grey Corries, the mountains of Glencoe and Ben Cruachan. ◄

Beyond the stile, the service track climbs quite steeply in places until it zigzags round to the rear of the first two **radio masts**.

The broad track divides. Take the right branch and follow it as it winds up onto **Maol nan Uan**, where there is another radio mast, sheltered by a low bluff. Climb up onto this, soon passing the small Loch Maol nan Uan,

with Mainnir nam Fiadh in view ahead. A succession of easy rises leads upwards and westwards, roughly parallel with the cliff edge falling into Coire Mòr and Coire nan Each, and following a narrow but increasingly discernible path. The conditions underfoot are superb, short turf and a few spreads of rock, all of which makes for easy going as you climb to the trig pillar and huge cairn on **Mainnir nam Fiadh**.

133

Especially inviting is the long, undulating ridge that runs in a north-westerly direction over Beinn Thunacaraidh, Beinn Mheadhan and Beinn Chreagach Mhòr along the north-eastern flanks of Glen Forsa (Walk 2.15).

Dùn da Ghaoithe lies a short distance further on, reached across a narrow ridge of splendid turf and rock, rising finally at an easy angle to reach the summit, marked by a massive cairn. Not surprisingly, the view is outstanding, extending westwards across Beinn Talaidh to Ben More, a splendid rippling landscape of fine Mull summits. ◀

The simplest, safest and surest way down is now to retrace your steps, and this option should be exercised in poor visibility. There is no saving in overall distance, and there is a little more uphill as you climb back across Mainnir nam Fiadh, but this is by far the quickest and easiest way back.

The onward route, however, continues northwards from Dùn da Ghaoithe, descending immediately across rock and grass. In this direction lies a long, broad and mainly grassy ridge leading down to Beinn Chreagach, but your purpose is to circle around **Coire na Circe**, high above the Allt an Dubh-choire. Good visibility is need to ensure that the correct line is taken, especially so as to avoid heading out to Beinn Thunacaraidh. Once

Dùn da Ghaoithe – the final stretch

the correct line is assured, fairly easy walking follows, although there are a few brief rock bands to find a way through in the steeper upper section of the descent. After that, short grass and minor rock outcrops prevail for much of the time.

Gradually, however, you need to bear to the right, staying parallel with, but high above, the **Allt an Dubh-choire**. When you can pick out a deer fence above the river, you need to decide which way you choose to continue:

For the shorter route, saving about 2km (1½ miles), head down to the Allt an Dubh-choire, and follow it to meet a deer fence. Cross the river on boulders, and go through a gate in the fence. Then continue with the Allt an Dubh-choire, now on your left, until you meet a track beside the **Scallastle River**. ▶ Once you reach the track, turn through a gate and follow a rough stretch until you meet another track and a bridge spanning the Scallastle River. Over the bridge, climb into open woodland, keeping left at a junction. The onward route is a variable commodity as clear-felling has changed the landscape somewhat. But then better paths and tracks materialise as this is now part of an increasingly managed forest, specifically with the intention of encouraging walkers. The route is waymarked, and leads down to the forest car park opposite the entrance to the **Isle of Mull Hotel**.

For the longer alternative, keep above the Allt an Dubh-choire, and head down to the deer fence, through which there is a gate at NM686378. Through the gate, which is at a corner in a fence, now follow descending quad bike tracks that lead you on to walk along a forest edge above a ravine containing the **Allt na Criche**. The going is not easy, being wet, and, lower down, overgrown by bracken, but the route remains clear throughout. Eventually you descend to cross the burn, beyond which a better track appears. This leads steadily downwards through mainly birch and willow woodland and feeds into an old part of the highway, although it is seasonally overgrown. However, you can hear the traffic on the main road, and, when you feel able to do so, within

Conditions underfoot are unpleasant on the way to the Scallastle River, but the worst of it is short-lived.

sight (through trees) of the road, find an easy way through, emerging onto the A849 at **Alltcreich** (NM686391), opposite the entrance to the Scallastle Marine Farm. Now turn right, and follow the road back to **Craignure**, 4km (2½ miles) distant. You may, of course, decide to wait for a bus, which are fairly frequent along this route.

WALK 2.15
Dùn da Ghaoithe Ridge

Start	A849, south of Craignure (NM727349)
Finish	A849, near Pennygown cemetery
Distance	18.5km (11½ miles)
Total ascent	1075m (3525ft)
Terrain	Rough mountain upland, generally good underfoot in the first half, but with boggy interludes in the second half; not advised in poor visibility
Map	OS Explorer 375 Isle of Mull East: Craignure

The first part of this walk follows Walk 2.14 to the summit of Dùn da Ghaoithe, but as it is a linear walk you can be dropped off near the entrance to Torosay Castle, rather than walk from Craignure. The complete walk is a major undertaking, one of the finest ridge walks on Mull, and quite demanding in its latter stages when low cliffs and peat hags can prove tiring. To make matters worse, the end of the walk is increasingly affected by quarry workings, and may mean spending time trying to figure out a safe and easy way down to the A-road. These difficulties aside, on a fine walking day, with clear skies, the entire walk is as good as anything on Mull, and ranks favourably with many walks on mainland Scotland.

It is possible to tackle this walk using public transport, and services run frequently along the A849. It is even possible to get to the Torosay Castle start by using the narrow-gauge railway from Craignure.

The ascent to Dùn da Ghaoithe using Walk 2.14 is not unduly difficult, as it follows a radio station service road for some considerable distance before moving onto mountain ground. But it is easy to underestimate just how far it is, so, with the more difficult half still to come, when you reach the top of **Dùn da Ghaoithe**, you might want to re-assess your intentions.

Otherwise, set off northwards from Dùn da Ghaoithe summit, but very soon start to swing through north-west to west as you descend to a col before a short pull on to **Beinn Thunacaraidh**. The way onward dances up, over or around a series of minor hillocks and lochans as it crosses **Beinn Mheadhan** and then **Beinn Chreagach Mhòr**.

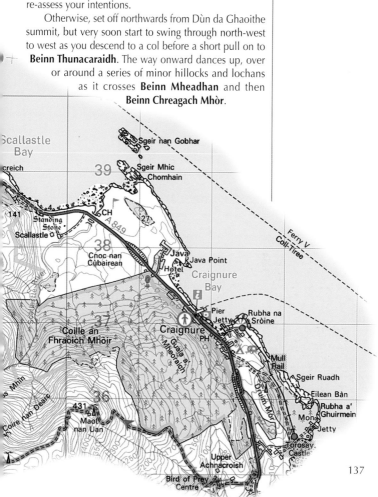

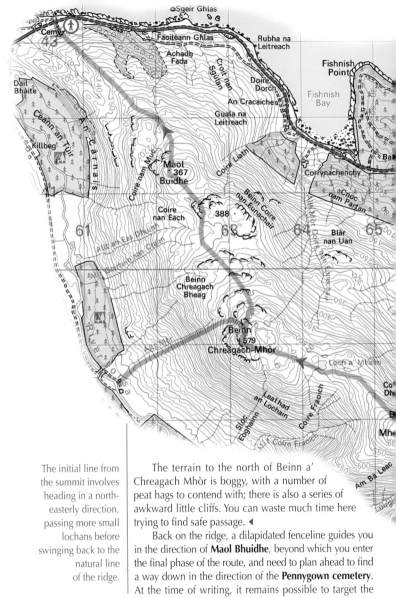

The initial line from the summit involves heading in a north-easterly direction, passing more small lochans before swinging back to the natural line of the ridge.

The terrain to the north of Beinn a' Chreagach Mhòr is boggy, with a number of peat hags to contend with; there is also a series of awkward little cliffs. You can waste much time here trying to find safe passage. ◄

Back on the ridge, a dilapidated fenceline guides you in the direction of **Maol Bhuidhe**, beyond which you enter the final phase of the route, and need to plan ahead to find a way down in the direction of the **Pennygown cemetery**. At the time of writing, it remains possible to target the cemetery and reach the A-road close by. But quarry workings, minor as they are, may affect the line chosen, and there is something to be said for heading down somewhere between north and east from Maol Bhuidhe to intercept an old road.

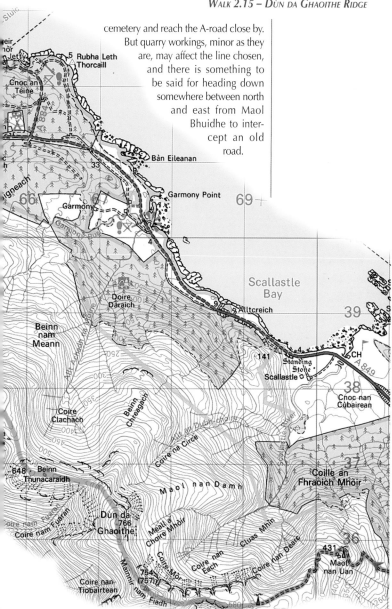

The summit of Dùn da Ghaoithe

Alternative descent via Glen Forsa
From a point to the north-west of Beinn a' Chreagach Mhòr, off the route described, it is possible to fashion a descent into Glen Forsa to the south-west, by heading for the sheep station at NM615384, from where you can access the main Glen Forsa track and walk out to Pennygown. But the descent requires care and lies in the opposite direction from the orthodox route along the ridge. It is possible to pick out a bracken- and largely trouble-free way down, although avoiding waterlogged ground will never be easy. ◀

Note that after this option, there is no further way down into Glen Forsa.

Ben Buie from Lochbuie

3 ROSS OF MULL

INTRODUCTION

For the purposes of this book, the Ross of Mull, which fundamentally is that long peninsula sandwiched between Loch Scridain and the Firth of Lorn, has been extended as far as Craignure, and embraces all the land to the south of the A849. This is a region that is 48km (30 miles) across, and most of it is traversed by only a single-track road. That in itself holds great appeal – you can go nowhere in a hurry – almost forcing visitors to take in the landscape, which is nothing short of magnificent.

Immediately south of Craignure, Torosay Castle and Duart Castle stand guard either side of Duart Bay, while the seemingly innocuous Grass Point on the edge of Loch Don, holds a special place in the history of Mull, for it was from here that cattle were taken across to the mainland, and where pilgrims bound for Iona used to alight. This whole area was once well populated, as the ruins at Gualachaolish testify. This remote settlement, now inhabited mainly by red deer, and the stubby finger of the Croggan peninsula, almost land-lock the sheltered Loch Spelve, renowned these days for its excellent mussels.

At Strathcoil, a narrow road runs south through the most delightful countryside to reach Lochbuie, a one-way road that leads on beyond Loch Uisg to Moy Castle and the great bay of Loch Buie. For walkers this is remote country, a place where rugged mountains – Ben Buie and Beinn na Gobhar – rise abruptly from the sea, and coastal paths – between Lochbuie and Malcolm's Point beyond Carsaig – provide some of the most entertaining and challenging walking on the island.

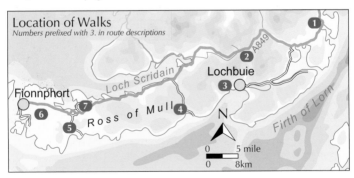

Location of Walks
Numbers prefixed with 3. in route descriptions

Gleann a' Chaiginn Mhòir

The Ross of Mull, of course, is the key to reaching Iona. But the long and seemingly endless drive to Fionnphort is one that should be savoured not hastened over. Diverging excursions from the main road take the curious north into the sanctuary of Mull's highest mountains, and south, out along minor, twisting roads, to places like Ardalanish and the tidal island of Erraid, where David Balfour in Robert Louis Stevenson's *Kidnapped* landed and spent four days before realising that, as we can do, it was possible simply to walk off the island at low tide. Most visitors are bound for Iona, but there is a fine ramble around the Ardtun headland east of Loch na Làthaich, not far from the village of Bunessan.

Here along the Ross will be found some of Mull's wildest landscapes, rugged glens, smooth-sided hills that are an equal part in the harmonies of Mull.

WALK 3.1
Gualachaolish and Carn Ban

Start/Finish	A849, south of Lochdon (NM720318); limited parking beside gate; more parking further along road
Distance	Gualachaolish 8km (5 miles); Carn Ban 9km (5½ miles)
Total ascent	Gualachaolish 270m (885ft); Carn Ban 370m (1215ft)
Terrain	Open heath and upland; paths to Gualachaolish are often wet; route to Carn Ban is pathless
Map	OS Explorer 375 Isle of Mull East: Craignure

There is a better than average chance of seeing red deer on this out-and-back walk, and possibly wild goats, too. But its real purpose is to visit the ruins of the 19th-century house built as a manse for the minister of the parish of Torosay, and, if desired, to ascend Carn Ban. The entire walk traverses a landscape that is poorly drained, and so, other than after a prolonged dry spell, the ground and paths are waterlogged. But this should deter no-one properly clad, and the walk gives fine views over Loch Spelve and to the mountains north of Glen More.

The Auchnacraig peninsula is a beautiful area and a reminder that many parts of Mull are both farmland and important habitats for flora and fauna, often, as here, reflected in SSSI status. ▶

Pass through the gate and onto a grassy track, initially running beside a fence and wall, but then breaking free to strike across rough ground. The path is clear throughout the walk, making its way through a hummocky landscape, and leading to a padlocked gate at NM722305. Beyond, the track continues to a **ford** at NM718299, which can usually be leapt across easily enough, but which, even in spate, is unlikely to call for much of a diversion.

After the ford, the path climbs for a while to a high point at NM716297, just below Maol an t-Searraich.

Gualachaolish

Walkers heading for Gualachaolish (pronounced Gool-a-cool-ish) should simply continue along the path, which undulates mildly onwards to pass through a wall at NM714293 that marks the boundary of the crofting land beyond, now largely given over to bracken. Ahead and below you can see the ruins of Killean graveyard to which coffins were brought by boat from Croggan and the more distant Lochbuie. The ruins of Gualachaolish lie another 400m along the track. From here simply retrace your outward route.

Carn Ban

Those heading for the Marilyn, Carn Ban, in poor visibility, need to be competent navigators. There is no path, and large swathes of chest-high bracken to contend with, but by leaving the main path at the high point (NM716297), and choosing a line that avoids as much as possible of the bracken, you can find a way steadily upwards. The summit lies beyond transverse grassy ridges and hummocks that confuse navigation, but which are easy enough, in a free-range roaming kind of way, to cross. The summit is marked by a trig pillar.

If conditions are favourable, you can strike south-west from the summit, aiming for Gualachaolish, but will need to plot a route that

Auchnacraig is an important environment for birdlife, deer and goats, and, here, as elsewhere, walkers are reminded to act responsibly. Please look out for any guidance during the stalking season.

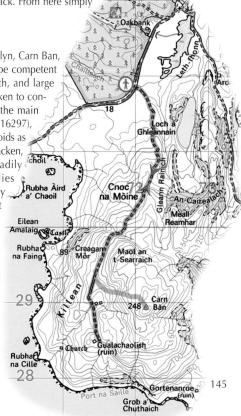

Carn Ban and Loch Spelve

evades the clutches of bracken that lie in that direction. A line that is rather more westerly will prove a little easier, again crossing transverse grassy ridges and minor hills, targeting the wall and path junction at NM714293.

On a fine day, it is a considerable delight to explore this now wild corner of Mull. But once explored the simplest return route is to relocate the path used on the outward leg and go back along it.

WALK 3.2

Glen More to Lochbuie

Start	Head of Glen More, on A849 (NM616303)
Finish	Lochbuie (NM608249)
Distance	7km (4½ miles)
Total ascent	75m (50ft)
Total descent	285m (935ft)
Terrain	Rough and wet glen paths; rugged terrain; fords
Map	OS Explorer 375 Isle of Mull East: Craignure

The three lochs that are a feature of this walk are eye-catching and a popular photo stop for visitors. From the safety of the Glen More road, they are attractive and appealing, a characteristic sustained by closer acquaintance. But this is rarely a dry walk, and the sense of remoteness, in the shadow of towering Ben Buie, is keen throughout. As with all linear walks, the issue of transport needs to be resolved. Buses operate along Glen More, but not so to Lochbuie. Strong walkers could consider retracing the route and walking back to Glen More, but to do so puts a fair amount of rough and rugged ascent into the return journey, something that is lacking when heading for Lochbuie, as the general trend is downwards.

Leave the A849 at its highest point, where a vehicle track descends towards the three lochs. The track does not help you for long, as it takes the line of (probably) the old road through the glen. Before long you need to leave this, and strike out for the lochs, keeping as high as possible to avoid the worst of the wet ground, but your target is the burn that links **Loch an Ellen** and **Loch Airde Glais**. There is a tempting quad bike track that keeps to the west of Loch Airde Glais that may help (but this has not been walked by the author).

Instead, you need to ford the burn linking the two lochs, beyond which a long-established path presses on to the col, boggy it is has to be said, at the head of

Gleann a' Chaiginn Mhòir

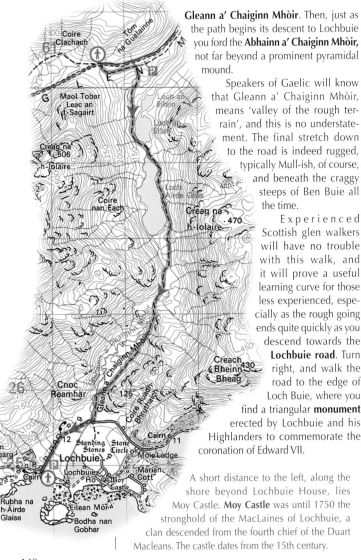

Gleann a' Chaiginn Mhòir. Then, just as the path begins its descent to Lochbuie you ford the **Abhainn a' Chaiginn Mhòir,** not far beyond a prominent pyramidal mound.

Speakers of Gaelic will know that Gleann a' Chaiginn Mhòir, means 'valley of the rough terrain', and this is no understatement. The final stretch down to the road is indeed rugged, typically Mull-ish, of course, and beneath the craggy steeps of Ben Buie all the time.

Experienced Scottish glen walkers will have no trouble with this walk, and it will prove a useful learning curve for those less experienced, especially as the rough going ends quite quickly as you descend towards the **Lochbuie road.** Turn right, and walk the road to the edge of Loch Buie, where you find a triangular **monument** erected by Lochbuie and his Highlanders to commemorate the coronation of Edward VII.

A short distance to the left, along the shore beyond Lochbuie House, lies Moy Castle. **Moy Castle** was until 1750 the stronghold of the MacLaines of Lochbuie, a clan descended from the fourth chief of the Duart Macleans. The castle dates from the 15th century.

The whole of the final stage of the walk, like the village of Lochbuie itself, is dominated by the mass of Ben Buie, a formidable mountain viewed from this angle.

Walkers with the energy and inclination may, on reaching the road by the bridge over the Abhainn a' Chaiginn Mhòir, go through a gate opposite and follow a path that leads round to Mull's only remaining **stone circles**, the most pronounced of which comprises nine stones with a few outliers.

WALK 3.3

Lochbuie to Carsaig

Start	Lochbuie (NM608249)
Finish	Carsaig (NM544215)
Distance	8.5km (5¼ miles)
Total ascent	370m (1215ft)
Terrain	Coastal walking, some of it rugged; a short section using a fixed rope; woodland
Map	OS Explorer 375 Isle of Mull East: Craignure

The walk from Lochbuie to Carsaig is one of the finest coastal sections on Mull, but it is no easy stroll, and will embrace scrambling among boulders, especially at high tide, a section of raised beach and a stretch of woodland. At one point the only onward way is to resort to a length of fixed rope in order to get down (easily enough) a short cliff. Along the way you may encounter evidence of past attempts to construct a shore route between the two settlements, given that the road route between them is 41km (25½ miles). The walk is interesting throughout its length, one of considerable contrast and short enough for strong walkers to consider turning round and walking back, thus resolving the transport logistics.

The Loch Buie coastline to Carsaig

The walk begins easily enough, following a good track from the shore at Lochbuie as far as Glenbyre Farm. Long before this, the road surfacing ends, and you encounter a bridge where the track divides. Ignore the turning to Cameron Farm, and keep to the left-hand, lower track which leads on to **Glenbyre**. Just beyond the farm, a

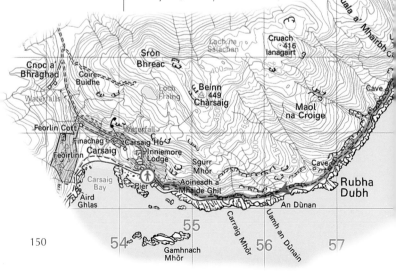

bridge spans **Glenbyre Burn**, and you wander on into a fairly lush landscape, sheltered and tranquil, and a marked contrast with what now follows. ▸ Walkers looking for an easy day might consider turning round at Glenbyre and retracing the route. It really is quite agreeable and straightforward.

Beyond Glenbyre, you tussle with rocks and boulders, and progress really slows. At one point, An Cui'-Leim, there is an awkward moment when you have to negotiate the descent of a 3m cliff; in dry conditions this should faze no one, but for many years a

The fecund vegetation is no chance thing; until the Clearances this was some of the best managed and fertile land on the island, and known locally as the Garden of Mull.

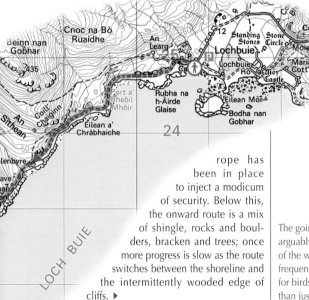

rope has been in place to inject a modicum of security. Below this, the onward route is a mix of shingle, rocks and boulders, bracken and trees; once more progress is slow as the route switches between the shoreline and the intermittently wooded edge of cliffs. ▸

An Dùnan is an isolated stack, and from here to Carsaig you cross the finest section of the walk, with the path now much better defined. This is a spectacular stretch where shallow caves proliferate, carved by the sea when its level was clearly much higher than today.

The going here is arguably the hardest of the walk, and frequent halts to look for birds are more than justified.

Once you enter woodland, the end is not far. There are some muddy sections through the trees, but now you are following a clear path that leads unerringly all the way to the pier and roadhead at **Carsaig**. Hopefully someone is there to collect you, although there is something to be said for following the minor road out through Glen Leidle to the Ross of Mull A-road at **Pennyghael** from where you can catch a bus back to Craignure. The walking is easy, of course, and the scenery quite special and worthy of the effort. This will add about 6km (3½ miles) to the walk distance.

The Lochbuie memorial

WALK 3.4

Carsaig Arches

Start/Finish	Carsaig (NM544215) – limited parking at road end
Distance	13km (8 miles)
Total ascent	350m (1150ft)
Terrain	Rocky, rugged coastal landscape; sea cliffs; boulders, shingle and rocks
Map	OS Explorer 373 Iona, Staffa and Ross of Mull

The walk to the Carsaig arches is one of the most stunning excursions on Mull, an experience that is constantly interesting and rugged, contrasting and demanding, and that cannot be wholly completed other than at low tide. So, consult the tide table before setting off. The arches themselves are spectacular formations and inevitably, one day, will collapse; they are part of an eroded sea cliff and as hugely impressive as the cliffs from which they are fashioned. The scenery is the result of erosion of the sedimentary rocks underlying the more widespread lava flows. Expect to encounter wild goats, golden and sea eagles and, in season, breeding fulmars and kittiwakes. Although popular, the walk is not one to do alone; it involves uneven ground, scrambling about on boulders, and narrow paths across vertiginous drops.

From the pier in Carsaig, walk back to the surfaced lane, and then take a track leading to the shoreline of **Carsaig Bay**. You soon encounter a fence, and here it is easier if you descend to walk along the shore; this makes it simpler to cross a couple of burns that lurk a short way ahead. Once beyond this little hiatus and onto the western side of the bay, the path improves and leads on to a feature known as the **Nun's Pass** or Nun's Cave ▶ , the only spot where the cliffs that accompany this walk are even remotely breached. Wide and shallow, and formed of sandstone topped with basalt, the cave was used by

The cave, well worth a brief diversion, is said to be the place where nuns evicted from Iona took refuge during the Reformation.

153

stonemasons working in a nearby quarry to extract sandstone until the late 19th century.

As the crow flies, the on-going distance to the Carsaig arches is not significant, but progress is very slow. There has been some damage to the path here, but ways round it,

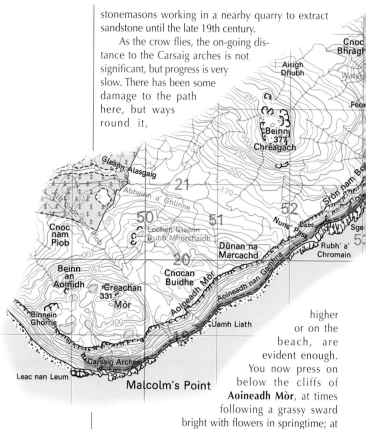

higher or on the beach, are evident enough. You now press on below the cliffs of **Aoineadh Mòr**, at times following a grassy sward bright with flowers in springtime; at other times you find yourself among the rocks and pebbles on the beach.

Eventually you round a corner and the first **arch** rises before you. Cross the beach towards it and climb onto a basalt outcrop. An inlet then bars further progress in that direction. To get any further you need to backtrack a little to a small burn and look for a goat track that takes you very precariously above the inlet – no place for any but the sure-footed. So, take no risks.

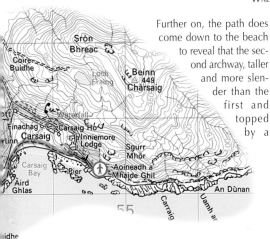

Further on, the path does come down to the beach to reveal that the second archway, taller and more slender than the first and topped by a chimney-like stack, is linked to the landward cliff by a natural, rocky causeway. It is a magnificent freak of Nature, a tower 36m (118ft) high, with a huge hole, not unlike a giant keyhole, through its middle. The base of the rock is Cretaceous, from the period of geological time, 145 million to 65 million years ago, during which the dinosaurs became extinct, while the upper part of the rock is basalt.

The safest return is now by your outward route.

The coastline at Carsaig

WALK 3.5

Ardalanish

Start/Finish	Ardalanish car park (NM373193)
Distance	5km (3 miles)
Total ascent	115m (380ft)
Terrain	Moorland tracks; and wild moorland devoid of tracks
Map	OS Explorer 373 Iona, Staffa and Ross of Mull

Quite how far you go with this walk is optional. The complete trek, down to Rudh' Ardalanish is not easy once you leave an otherwise excellent farm track, in fact, it is arduous, and so there is wisdom in contenting yourself with a simple and relaxing stroll among the hillocks of this southerly peninsula. Equally, from the car park at the start you can wander down a track to Ardalanish Bay. It is possible to walk along the bay and eventually find a way up through cliffs to the track above, but this is awkward and uncomfortable in places, and can be affected by the state of the tide.

Ardalanish Farm is completely organic, and has a working weaving mill fabricating a wide range of garments, rugs and throws using wool produced at the farm and from Lochtan sheep from the Isle of Man. The mill is open to visitors. Plans to open a café in 2008 were delayed, but it should be operating from 2010. If you are intending to walk the headland, then use the first car park, not the one at the mill.

Turn left out of the car park and follow the road to the mill, climbing beyond that to a large white house. Here, bear left on an unmade track, and, when it divides, pass through a gate, continuing to climb as the track sweeps round to farm outbuildings. Bear left here, still following a broad track that suddenly pitches you into an impressive landscape of hills and dales. On the way you pass a small blackhouse roofed with turf. Continue with the path, which leads on to a gate in a wall.

Pressing on, you head for the volcanic plug that hosts Dun Luachrach. For most walkers this will be far enough, as the continuation to Rubh' Ardalanish is anything but easy. If so, simply retrace your steps.

Extension to headland

There are no significant paths leading southwards to Rubh' Ardalanish, only discontinuous sheep tracks. Good navigating is needed, along with stamina, as the going can be tiring in places, the Mull landscape having reverted to type. A line to the west of Torr na Sealga is wisest, all bracken and heather. The going is difficult throughout this section, but eventually you locate the trig pillar that marks the headland, the southernmost point of Mull. Now all you have to do is find your way back.

The Ardalanish peninsula

WALK 3.6

Tireragan and Tràigh Gheal

Start/Finish	Knockvologan (NM316201); limited parking
Distance	8.5km (5¼ miles) – round trip
Total ascent	220m (720ft)
Terrain	Heather moorland, poorly drained in places
Map	OS Explorer 373 Iona, Staffa and Ross of Mull

This walk typifies what is so enjoyable about low-level walking on Mull. At times, the walking is a little challenging, not because of any fierce ascent or rugged cliffs, but because of the combined efforts of bracken, birch and willow to obstruct easy progress by snapping at your heels or by creating boggy patches for you to dance around or flounder through. That aside – a comparatively minor irritant – the landscape is wholly delightful throughout; bright in summer with yellow iris, valerian, loosestrife, devil's bit scabious, and richly purpled by heather later in the year.

At all times, please park considerately; this is an active farming community.

There is limited roadside parking at or just before the farm buildings at Knockvologan, just before a gate across the road. Do not continue to the end of the road. ◀

Pass through a gate between farm buildings (sign-posted 'Walks', and a box of leaflets nearby about Tireragan), and head along a track, initially stony but later carpeted with silverweed to reach a deer fence, beyond which you swing right onto lovely heather moorland, with a fine view to your left (north-east) of Ben More.

The path leads to a bridge and a deer gate/fence, after which the path divides. Fork left, and enjoy the easy pull onto **Torr Fada**. A clear path runs across the top of Torr Fada, mainly through heather, to an undistinguished summit (save for its magnificent all-round panorama),

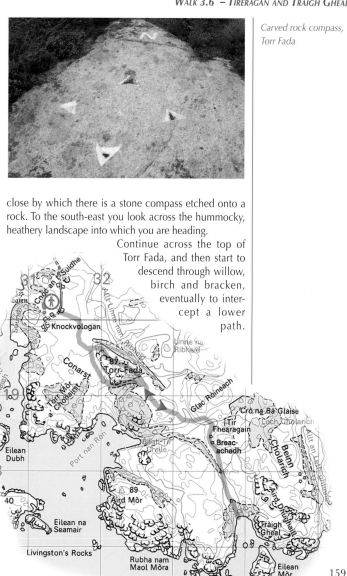

Carved rock compass, Torr Fada

close by which there is a stone compass etched onto a rock. To the south-east you look across the hummocky, heathery landscape into which you are heading.

Continue across the top of Torr Fada, and then start to descend through willow, birch and bracken, eventually to intercept a lower path.

159

TIRERAGAN

The wider estate of Tireragan, or in Gaelic Tìr Fhearagain (the 't' is pronounced as ch), is an area of great conservation significance, and since 1994 has been managed by a charity, Highland Renewal (Bendoran Cottage, Bunessan, Isle of Mull. Tel: 01681 700593; email: info@highlandrenewal. org; www.highlandrenewal.org), with the aim of regenerating the woodlands and other habitats for their amenity and educational value.

The estate is a truly splendid place, exhibiting the four main habitats of upland Britain: heath, woodland, mire (bog) and grassland. At its most basic, founded on the ancient Ross of Mull pink granite, the scenery is beautiful; a closer inspection reveals a wide diversity of plant life, especially lichens, mosses and liverworts. Elsewhere, iris, primrose and orchids are seasonally abundant.

Like numerous places among the islands of Scotland, the widespread township of Tireragan has a darker side. In the early 19th century, more than 100 souls eked out a living here, surviving on subsistence farming and what little income could be gained from the gathering and burning of seaweed to produce ash, which in turn was used in making gunpowder. Within a generation, kelp production became unprofitable, a situation made worse by potato blight, which completely wiped out the primary food source of the people. Then, when sheep farming became a more profitable use of land, a period of eviction followed, characterised by a policy of abuse, intimidation and unjustified and harsh evictions. By 1861, no-one remained at Tireragan or the nearby village of Breac-achadh. The remains of five settlements in all, their ruined cottages, walls and lazybed fields are a poignant reminder of these harsh times. The stone-built cottages probably date from the 18th and 19th centuries, as before the mid-18th century buildings were made of earth and wattle.

Turn left along this, initially easterly, and then southerly, as the path passes on across the moors of **Tireragan** (or Tìr Fhearagain, as it is known in Gaelic).

The on-going track brings you to a bridge at NM333186, after which the path swings to the left to avoid marshy ground. Once drier ground is attained, you can deviate to the east a little to visit the ruins of Tìr Fhearagain, or continue along the path, when you will soon pass the ruins of **Breac Achadh**.

Gnarled tree, Tireragan

The path now crosses to the opposite side of this low valley, and pitches you into a squabble with invasive bracken, and the more welcome birch thickets that are essential to the future well-being of this reserve. This stretch, leading eventually down to the beach, is the most demanding and trying, but persistence will bring you to a steepish incline, following a continuous path descending through widespread birch that you will have to push a way through, to reach **Tràigh Gheal**, a beautiful spot that many regard as the finest and most secluded beach on Mull. ▶

That the beach is so awkward to reach makes it all the more appealing.

You need to retrace your steps now to Knockvologan. The only change in route occurs as you reach the foot of the path coming down from Torr Fada. Instead of climbing back over the hill, you can go forward on a clear path into another heathery valley, from which the path does eventually rise onto the shoulder of Torr Fada. Simply keep following this path and it will return you, fairly uneventfully, to the deer gate/fence you passed through earlier in the walk.

WALK 3.7

Ardtun

Start/Finish	Lower Ardtun (NM383231)
Distance	*Aoineadh Mòr* 4km (2½ miles); circuit 6.5km (4 miles)
Total ascent	*Aoineadh Mòr* 70m (230ft); circuit 125m (410ft)
Terrain	Coastal margins; rough moorland
Map	OS Explorer 373 Iona, Staffa and Ross of Mull

Both the shorter and the longer of these two splendid short walks is capable of waylaying intentions, not least because the sheltered waters of Loch na Làthaich are popular with wildlife, but also because the geology of the area, possessing a fascinating array of small basalt columns, is enough to eat into time. This is not a place of dramatic sea cliffs, surging seas or oceanic vistas; it is more prosaic than that, a delight, an easy stroll, a potter. On a fine day, take a picnic and a pair of binoculars, and settle among the ruined crofts of Aoineadh Mòr. Ardtun is a stubby peninsula north of Bunessan, and to the east of Loch na Làthaich. Its exploration is easy, and the walks here perfect for a lazy half day or when higher ground is shrouded in mist.

There is room to park a few cars near the road junction at Lower Ardtun, and from here you set off down the road, alongside **Traig Mhòr**. Continue past **Eorabus**, and then, as the road makes a pronounced bend to the left, leave on the apex by passing through a gate into a pasture (NM380237). Go forward towards a low outcrop, beyond which you walk beside a wall and fence on a narrow, grassy path to a gap in a corner.

Once through the gap there are two possibilities: one is to take a low-level path, on-going, that more or less follows the coastline; the other is to bear a little to the right onto slightly higher, and drier, ground heading for

Basalt columns, Aoineadh Mòr

the conspicuous Dùnan Mòr, a rocky upthrust crowned by a cairn. You will need to step over a fence on the way, but can do so without damage or injury.

Beyond Dùnan Mòr there are vague paths, but by sticking with the coastline you can eventually reach the scattered, ruined crofts at Aoineadh Mòr. Close by, at water level, there is a fine display of basalt columns, smaller, less upright and more recumbent than on Staffa.

Abandoned croft, Aoineadh Mòr

Gradually, the dramatic headland of Ardmeanach comes into view, bold sweeps of vertiginous cliffs and waterfalls; this is Mull's wild landscape at its best.

Those just wanting a short walk now need only retrace their steps. Otherwise, press on along the shoreline, keeping below low cliffs, using sheep tracks to pass them, and walk on through heather. Avoid going too high onto the moor, which is rather wet. ◄

Cross a fence, and carry on, keeping seaward of the hillock, Tòrr an Locha, to reach a gap in a wall, and then continue across the top of a grassy ravine running down to a small beach. Head for a gate in a wall, and then keep to the right of a dilapidated wall with Loch a' Chrionain in view to your right.

Next you encounter a gated track, which passes a **cottage** and enters a small woodland before becoming surfaced. Now simply follow the lane out to a T-junction, and turn right to return to **Lower Ardtun**.

Camas Cùil an t-Saimh, Iona

4 THE ISLANDS

INTRODUCTION

Mull is not one island, but a group of islands, only one of which, Calve Island, is to the east, sheltering the harbour of Tobermory. Few of the islands – Erraid, Erisgeir, Inch Kenneth, Iona, Eorsa, Little Colonsay, Staffa, Ulva, Gometra and the Treshnish Isles – are large enough, or sufficiently easy of access to warrant inclusion in a guidebook for walkers. These are gathered in the south-west between the Treshnish headland and the end of the Ross of Mull.

Of those not included in this book, the Treshnish Isles and Staffa are accessible as non-residential tourist destinations during the summer months, and are well worth visiting for their geology and natural history, but do not yield walks of any length; in any case, the call of the ferry means that time on the islands is limited.

STAFFA AND THE TRESHNISH ISLES

Staffa is renowned for Fingal's Cave, a magnificent geological cave of basalt columns linked beneath the waves to the Giant's Causeway in County

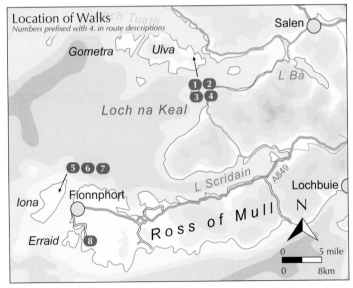

Antrim in Northern Ireland. The naturalist Thomas Pennant, who visited this part of Scotland in 1772, does indeed describe Staffa as 'a new Giant's Causeway, rising amidst the waves; but with columns of double the height of that in Ireland; glossy and resplendent, from the beams of the eastern sun.' For him, unable to land, it was nevertheless a 'wondrous isle'.

Everyone should visit Staffa at least once. It was made famous by the composer Felix Mendelssohn in his Hebrides Overture, the musical theme of which is commonly known as 'Fingal's Cave'. The artist Turner made the island the subject of an oil painting; accompanied by dramatic sketches it appears alongside text in Walter Scott's *The Lord of the Isles*, and has been described in prose and verse by Wordsworth, Keats, Tennyson and others.

Further north, the Treshnish Isles are magnificent places in spring and summer, teeming with birdlife and riddled with burrows from which puffin appear at your feet before darting off in search of more food for their young.

ULVA AND GOMETRA

The sizeable island of Ulva is a mere 150m from mainland Mull, and reached by a small ferry that has been running for as long as anyone can remember. Visitors are welcome on Ulva (see pages 20–21 for details of the seasonal ferry timings).

The lavic terraces of which the island is composed give Ulva, the largest of the Mull islands, a squat wedding-cake profile, distinctive and visible from afar. The lush summer greenness of bracken conceals a fine-grained igneous rock that at the south-eastern end gives way to mini-versions of the basaltic columns found on Staffa. Little disturbs the peace of Ulva; with no roads to speak of, there are no cars, only the quad bikes used by those that live here, and nothing to detract from what Mairi Hedderwick describes as an 'ambling ambience of an island preserved in aspic'.

When the travelling twosome Johnson and Boswell visited Ulva in 1773, they were advised that 'there was nothing worthy of observation', and they did not stay long. But on this island, 12 years earlier, had been born one Lachlan Macquarie, who went on to serve in the British Army, rising to become a Major-General; for 10 years from 1810 he served as Governor-General of New South Wales in Australia, and did so with considerable distinction and compassion, qualities that earned him lasting respect, as evidenced by the preponderance of features, buildings, streets and institutions in Australia that still bear his name to this day. But it also earned him a measure of unfair criticism, and eventually he was brought back to England. Macquarie's efforts saw New South Wales transformed from a degenerate colony of convicts to one that was prosperous and well

Sheila's Cottage, Ulva

administered. His work earned him the epithet 'The Father of Australia'. He died on Mull in 1824, and his body lies in a mausoleum at Gruline, preserved by the National Trust for Scotland on behalf of the National Trust of Australia.

Across Ulva today you find evidence of the former crofting communities, notably along the rough track that leads to Gometra, and along the south coast to Ormaig, probable birthplace of Macquarie, and Cragaig. Here, too, is a croft lived in by the grandparents of explorer David Livingstone. In the 19th century, more than 600 people lived on Ulva, most of them involved in producing kelp ash. But when the market collapsed, closely followed by potato blight, the landowner decided that the only solution to the resultant

destitution was to clear the land and give it over to sheep. Between 1846 and 1851, he deported more than two-thirds of the population, evicting families in a ruthless manner, setting fire to the thatch of their cottages, and denying his tenants even so much as the chance to retrieve what few possessions they had. Today, the population barely reaches double figures.

At the far end of Ulva, the island of Gometra is separated from Ulva by a narrow cleft, spanned by a single arch bridge which continues the rough track from Ulva ferry to Gometra House and the west coast anchorage, Acairseid Mhòr. This tiny island was sometime home to Hugh Ruttledge, renowned Himalayan explorer and leader of the unsuccessful 1933 expedition to Everest.

IONA

Iona was here first; its rocks of Lewisian gneiss are among the oldest in Britain, indeed in the world. On this foundation, overlain in the east by later Torridonian sediments, rests Iona. To casual study, Iona seems to have been a geological afterthought, tacked on to Mull; in reality it was the other way round.

Commonly associated, through the work of St Columba, with the introduction of Christianity to Scotland – in which regard the island must defer to Whithorn, in Dumfries and Galloway, where the wandering St Ninian worked among a Christian community at least 100 years earlier – the island of Iona will draw everyone who has a love of the outdoors. It is a magical isle, ringed by beaches of golden-sand and craggy shorelines, blessed with a hearty moorland of hummocks and hollows, and with a tiny, but almost magisterial hill, Dun I.

During his 34 years on Iona, Columba did indeed use it as a base from which to mastermind an evangelical crusade, one that extended beyond the island, and beyond Scotland into Europe. So revered is the island that more than 40 Scottish kings lie buried here, alongside four kings of Ireland, eight kings of Norway, and one unknown king of France, who abdicated and came to Iona to die. Yet for the long-distance walker, the backpacker, the mountaineer, the seekers of city lights, there is nothing here, unless one's expectations are moderated, and sublimated into a contentment with a place of

Iona abbey cloisters

Sailing across the Sound of Iona

peace and tranquillity, where the wonders of Nature far exceed those of Men, whatever their shades of piety.

Iona is not for the hasty or the heedless, but is a realm where you can be at one with Nature, and with yourself. Visitors aplenty from across the world pour from the ferry and turn right into an island whose economy they support. But the real appeal of Iona is, as Thomas Pennant described, its 'little rocky hills, with narrow verdant hollows between (for they merit not the name of valleys) and numerous enough for every recluse to take his solitary walk, undisturbed by society.' Iona is for the hushed observer; the listener to the winds; the calm mind of silent reason.

ERRAID

Accessible at low tide by a tramp across Erraid Sound, this tiny island of heathery hummocks and mildly boggy hollows is a delight. Robert Louis Stevenson spent part of his youth here; his father, an engineer employed by the Board of the Northern Lights, used the island to quarry stones with which to build the Skerryvore Lighthouse south-west of Tiree and the one at Dhu Heartach.

Stevenson wove the island into his story of David Balfour, *Kidnapped*, in which the hapless shipwreck spent four days on the island, watching for help to the west, unaware that the island was tidal and easily accessible from the east.

WALK 4.1

Livingstone Croft Trail

Start/Finish	The Boathouse, Ulva (NM444397)
Distance	8.5km (5¼ miles)
Total ascent	295m (965ft)
Terrain	Undulating rock and heather moorland; low-level coastal walking; woodland
Map	OS Explorer 374 Isle of Mull North and Tobermory

This walk is simply quite delightful every step of the way, although getting beyond the refreshments and home-made cakes on offer at The Boathouse (a successful enterprise in the Local Food Heroes campaign) may prove a stumbling block. Ulva is a private island, not accessible on Saturdays, or on Sundays during winter months. There are no vehicles on the island, other than an occasional farm vehicle, and you experience a remarkable sense of remoteness. Getting there is by a two-minute ride on a small ferry that operates on an on-demand basis. There is a sign on the Mull side of the ferry that you can adjust to let the ferryman know that you are waiting.

This walk wanders through the woodlands, headlands and valleys of Ulva around the upthrust that is A' Chrannag. On the way you will pass the ruin of a cottage believed to have been occupied by relatives of the renowned explorer, David Livingstone. But the walk is really about the most delightful scenery, and, although there are shortcuts, it clings as long as possible to the coastline to wring every last ounce of pleasure from the day. There is a continuous path all the way, much of it waymarked.

The **ferry across to Ulva** from mainland Mull is of considerable antiquity, and is mentioned in the literature of 18th-century travellers, notably by Johnson and Boswell who visited Ulva in 1773, even if on their arrival at the ferry port, it was late in the day and the ferry had gone.

Leave The Boathouse and walk past the restored **Sheila's Cottage**, which is well worth visiting to get an idea of what living conditions used to be like – it is only a few strides from the path. After the cottage, walk on to a track junction, and take the one leading to the **church**. At the next junction, do likewise, continuing to head towards the church, which was built in 1827–28 to a design by Thomas Telford.

When you reach the church, note the interesting small, pyramidal war memorial.

◀ Now turn left, onto the 'Wood/Shore Walk', an ascending path into woodland. Above the woodland, the path breaks out into an open valley and then descends to a track junction. Here, turn right onto the 'Minister's Road', which promptly leads to a deer gate, and then traverses bracken and heather moorland.

In due course, the path intercepts the **main track** across the island, bound for Gometra, close by a large sheep pen. As you reach the main track, turn round to see the splendid Eas Fors waterfall on Mull, and then turn left to walk along the track.

When you reach a junction at NM428392, bear right on the track signposted for 'South Side' and 'Ormaig'.

The Boathouse

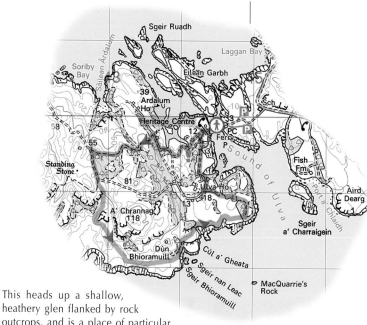

This heads up a shallow, heathery glen flanked by rock outcrops, and is a place of particular delight, with close-cropped turf underfoot. At NM424392, the main track continues around a heathery shoulder, towards South Side, but here, at a signpost, leave it by branching left onto the 'Livingstone Trail', which goes down initially beside a wall, descending into a partially wooded valley.

Continue down into birch woodland, which conceals lovely moss-covered wall. Below the woodland you break out to walk along a path overgrown with bracken, the route now being waymarked with white-topped poles.

The path eventually leads you down to the **Livingstone cottage**, once lived in by the ancestors of the explorer David Livingstone. The setting is quite special, and the outlook across Loch na Keal, a memorable one.

THE LIVINGSTONE CROFT

The Livingstones were descended from the Beaton family, the doctors of Pennyghael, physicians to the Lords of the Isles. David Livingstone's grandfather was a respected crofter here on Ulva before he and his family moved to Blantyre, where David was born in 1813.

Whether the Livingstone family ever saw the view from their Ulva croft as 'memorable' is unknown, bound to the land as they were by the constant hardships of subsistence living in an unyielding, if, to modern eyes, beautiful environment. There are more cottages nearby, the remnants of a typical Ulva settlement, of which there were once as many as 16. Most cottages would have had a cow for milk, grew a few crops of oats and potatoes in the familiar runrig system of cultivation – the remains of which can still be picked out in places – and maybe owned, or shared, a boat for fishing.

The Livingstone croft

Beyond the cottage, continue along the waymarked path through bracken, and press on following the waymarks, which guide you round the flanks of **A' Chrannag**, the craggy profile of which is a constant presence throughout this stage of the walk.

Basalt columns, Ulva

Eventually, you reach a branching path, signed for 'Cave'. This is said to be a cave where the grandfather of David Livingstone lived for a while, while building his croft. Archaeological investigation of the cave has revealed evidence of occupation as long ago as 8000 years.

A short way further on along the main path, another branching path takes you down to the water's edge for a view of the basaltic columns that grace this stretch of coastline.

Returning to the main path, passing on through a stand of alder, and pressing on along a superb path above these low cliffs, eventually to reach a signpost that makes good use of an old hay turner. Here, keep to the right, following the coastline, and soon bring **Ulva House** into view. ▸

Just after a metal gate, at another signpost, keep right past the turning up to Ulva House, and stay along the 'Wood/Shore Walk', which now follows a path between and wall and the shoreline, and soon crosses a section of

Ulva House was built in the 1950s to replace a former house destroyed by fire during renovation work. Little was saved of the original house.

salt marsh. Across this, you come to a ladder-stile spanning a wall, over which the path goes left, and appears to head into a spread of hazel. But avoid this, and instead bear right, to pass around the wood, and emerge on the other side.

The path continues across grassy pasture, but then re-enters woodland, eventually emerging to meet a broad track. Turn right along this, and in turn come to another track junction, at which you turn right, signposted for 'The Ferry', and soon return to the start.

WALK 4.2
Ormaig and Cragaig

Start/Finish	The Boathouse, Ulva (NM444397)
Distance	11km (7 miles)
Total ascent	450m (1475ft)
Terrain	Undulating rock and heather moorland; low-level coastal walking; woodland
Map	OS Explorer 374 Isle of Mull North and Tobermory

The island of Ulva is always a delight to explore, but being a private island is accessible, Saturdays excluded, only from mid-April to mid-October. This is out-and-back walk, and visits the coastal settlements of Cragaig and of Ormaig, birthplace of Lachlan Macquarie. The scenery throughout is superb, and the walking is nowhere difficult.

While it may seem, on arrival, that the island is swamped beneath bracken, the reality is that the flora and fauna here is remarkable, and offers a wide range of habitats that in turn produce more than 500 species of plants, many of which, like Grass of Parnassus and devil's-bit scabious, contrive to flourish in open patches amid the heather late into September. The island has been designated an Environmentally Sensitive Area for Argyll and the islands, as well as a national scenic area.

To begin the walk, go past The Boathouse and
Sheila's Cottage, a replica of the cottage of Sheila
MacFadyen, one of the last crofters of Ulva. At the first
junction take the track for Ormaig; at the second, take
the track signed for the **church**. Further on, take the turning signposted for 'South Side' and 'Livingstone's Croft',
and when the track is joined by another from the right,
keep ahead to arrive at the old farm. Here, turn right on
the track for South Side, climbing stonily through broad-

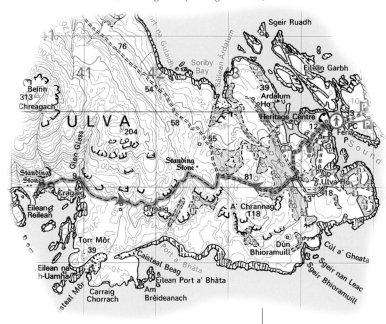

leaved woodland and past a small reservoir. Pass through
a deer gate, beyond which you break free of the woodland, and march out onto heath.

   Follow the track across the moorland, with slowly
improving views to the Ross of Mull and the Scottish
mainland beyond. Continue as far as NM429392, where
the main cross-island track for Gometra swings to the

Memorial, Ormaig view

The view from here is breathtaking, a host of tiny islets juxtaposed in perfect design so that in a certain light they look like a series of giant's stepping stones leading to the horizon.

right. Here, leave it, by turning left for South Side and Ormaig, with the on-going track soon curving round to enter a delightful, shallow heather valley. At the far end, the track climbs a little as it turns to pass the point of departure for anyone visiting the Livingstone Croft (Walk 4.1). Continue with the main track, climbing a little further to a high point at NM423390, where those heading for Beinn Chreagach (Walk 4.3) take their leave.

Press on across the high point, from which the track starts to descend towards **Ormaig**. On the way you reach a memorial cairn, with an inscription in French dated 8 December 2008. ◄

The path continues down to the abandoned crofts of Ormaig, above which there is another **memorial**. Popular opinion claims that Ormaig is the birthplace of Major-General Lachlan Macquarie, the Governor-General of

New South Wales in Australia, who now lies buried in a mausoleum at Gruline. But the memorial at Ormaig is not quite so adamant.

ULVA

Ulva was visited by Johnson and Boswell in 1773, but they didn't stay very long, and found Macquarie's home to be rather 'mean'. In 1841, the population of the island was 570; today it is 12 (of whom two attend school off the island). Three-quarters of the population were deported between 1846 and 1851 by the landowner, Francis William Clark. It was unfortunate that this was a time when the kelp industry, on which many of the islanders relied, foundered, and this was quickly followed by a period of severe potato blight. The result was that Ulva, at its height home to more than 600 crofters, was heavily over-populated. In fairness, Clark did try a number of relief schemes before arriving at the decision to clear the land, and he did pay a proportion of the costs of emigration. It was his employees rather than Clark himself, who, with or without his knowledge, forcibly evicted families from their cottages without warning, by putting torches to the thatch. They did not even allow time for the people to gather their few possessions, nor were they permitted to take their cattle, which were forfeit.

At the time of the evictions, one of the crofters owned a magnificent white horse. The factor, one of Clark's hated men, threatened that if the crofter did not take down the roof from his house, he would shoot the horse. The crofter refused, and the factor was true to his word and shot the horse. Incensed, the crofter pointed to a sapling growing nearby and predicted that when the sapling died, the family line of the proprietor, Clark, would also die out. He was almost right: some years later the sapling was struck by lightning, and one of the Clark family was killed in action in Italy during the Second World War, but the family line continued.

Beyond the Ormaig memorial, the path continues through bracken to reach the shore at **Cragaig**, where a solitary dwelling now serves as a bothy.

The whole of this coastal stretch is charming, laden with the sorrow of what happened to its people. No reward can ease the sadness of those dark days, but in small measure the beauty of what remains is, to a receptive mind, a token of compensation.

Ormaig

WALK 4.3
Beinn Chreagach

Start/Finish	The Boathouse, Ulva (NM444397)
Distance	12km (7½ miles)
Total ascent	400m (1310ft)
Terrain	Undulating rock and heather moorland
Map	OS Explorer 374 Isle of Mull North and Tobermory

Beinn Chreagach is the highest point of Ulva, and, like many high points, difficult to get to. With Beinn Chreagach, it is not a question of altitude, but of finding a way through a widespread cloak of bracken than in places is near impenetrable. Thanks are due, then, to Jamie Howard of Ulva, for this suggested approach; once on the hill itself there is no path, and you are left much to your own devices to work out a way forward that keeps bracken-bashing to a minimum.

Walk 4.2, bound for Ormaig and Cragaig, should be followed from The Boathouse as far as the high point at NM423390. Nothing distinguishes this point, save for the fact that the continuing path now falls away ahead of you, and a waymark post placed by the laird.

Leave the track and dive into the heather, working steadily upwards in a north-westerly direction to reach the end of a wall at NM419395. This wall will guide you up to a small **prominence** with a spot height of 204m. From here, you can plot a route up to the summit. The best line appears to lie initially to the north, but then swinging round to a westerly direction once you are due east of the summit. ◀

Beinn Chreagach is a Marilyn, and its summit marked is by a trig pillar. From here it is safest to retrace your steps.

There is no easy line, and such ways onward as may appear will vary according to the amount of seasonal overgrowth, but the island's owner has now waymarked a route to the summit.

WALK 4.4
Round Ulva

Start/Finish	The Boathouse, Ulva (NM444397)
Distance	19km (12 miles)
Total ascent	685m (2245ft)
Terrain	Good tracks to Cragaig and from Gometra; rough coastal moorland in between
Map	OS Explorer 374 Isle of Mull North and Tobermory

The walk around the island of Ulva is quite special, visiting first the deserted settlements of Ormaig and Cragaig before finding a way along the rough coastline of the south of the island, and heading for the bridge spanning the narrow inlet that links Ulva with its neighbour, Gometra. Once at the bridge, an easy walk returns you speedily to the ferry. But it is important to recognise that the entire walk is quite time-consuming, and that an early start and good progress needs to be made in order not to miss the last ferry back to Mull at 5pm or complete this outstanding walk in indecent haste. The manager of the island has indicated a willingness to waymark the stretch of the walk between Cragaig and the Gometra bridge, but at the time of writing (January 2010) this has yet to be completed.

The walk begins by following Walk 4.2 as far as the bothy at **Cragaig**. There are a few abandoned cottages here, their ruins a stark reminder of the harshness that befell the island.

There is a village graveyard a little to the south, towards the sea, where the graves of several of the Macquarie family will be found. ◄

Pass to the north of a couple of prominent **standing stones**, with fine seaward views dominated by a host of tiny islands popular with seals. Press on to the ruined village of Kilvekewan (**Cille Mhic Eoghainn** in Gaelic). ◄

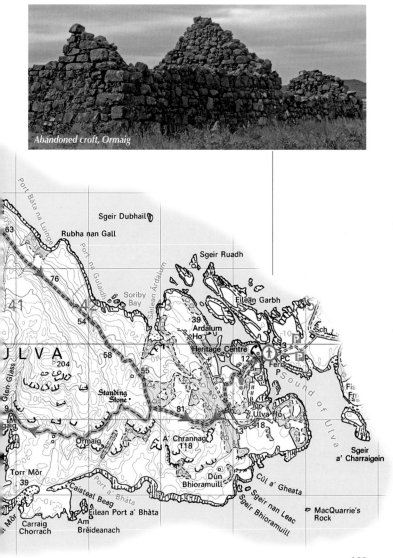

Abandoned croft, Ormaig

Beyond Kilvekewan, route finding is not easy, although it is essentially just a question of remaining below the cliffs of Beinn Eolasary and above those that fall to the sea.

The walk continues round the end of the island, passing what little remains on **Dun Isagain** before crossing rough ground to reach the **bridge** linking Ulva and Gometra. Now all that remains is the follow the broad and clear track back towards the Ulva ferry until you intercept the route used in the early stages of the walk (at NM428392).

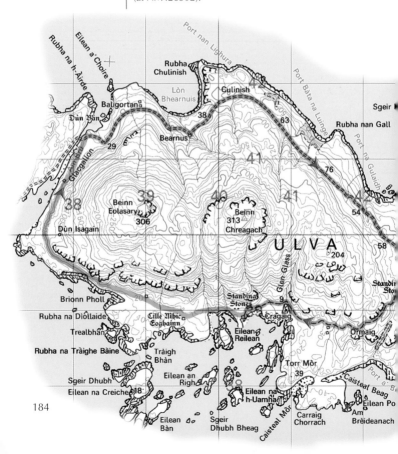

WALK 4.5

Gometra

Start/Finish	The Boathouse, Ulva (NM444397)
Distance	Gometra Bridge 17km (10½ miles); Gometra summit 26km (16¼ miles)
Total ascent	Gometra Bridge 290m (950ft); Gometra summit 570m (1870ft)
Terrain	Good tracks as far as Gometra; the ascent of Gometra is up broken rocky slopes
Map	OS Explorer 374 Isle of Mull North and Tobermory

Most walkers heading for Gometra should be satisfied with simply reaching the island at Gometra Bridge; that is a long enough walk in itself, and an entirely agreeable one almost entirely on a good, wide track that allows for speedy and easy progress. Anyone intending to go further, and climb to the top of Gometra, will find the extra effort worthwhile but demanding; there is still some way to go once you reach Gometra, and an early start is necessary if you are not to miss the last ferry (5pm).

The walk to Gometra is delightful every step of the way, and should be savoured. Walk 4.1 should be followed until it reaches the large sheep station NM427396, or use the early stages of Walk 4.2, then in both cases turn right along the broad trail that takes a delightful route around the island, finally reaching the bridge that links Ulva and Gometra. ◄ Once you reach the bridge, simply come back the same way. But allow for the fact that for many walkers this is a five-hour round trip.

With an early start, though, and a strong pair of legs, you can continue on to Gometra, where the track continues, later passing **Gometra House**, and pressing on northwards around the western coast of the island. There, if

This is splendid, leg-swinging walking, accompanied by lovely views across Loch Tuath to the Treshnish headland.

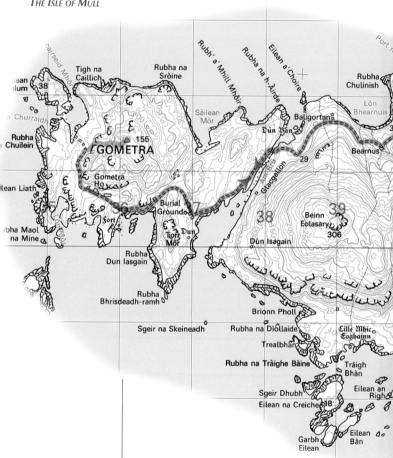

you want to climb to the high point of the island, marked
by a trig pillar, you can find a way up through rock outcrops, although there is no significant path to guide you.
Do not underestimate the time needed to complete this
walk. It means being on the first ferry across to the island,
and pressing on immediately if you are not to miss the
last ferry back.

If you followed Walk 4.1 on the way out, you can save a little time on the way back by continuing along the main track past the sheep station rather than branching left to retrace your entire outward route. Instead, go forward a little further to a track junction, at NM428392, and there turn left retracing the route used in Walk 4.2.

WALK 4.6

Dun I

Start/Finish	Iona ferry slip (NM286240)
Distance	3.5km (2 miles)
Total ascent	95m (310ft)
Terrain	Road walking; rugged hill moorland
Map	OS Explorer 373 Iona, Staffa and Ross of Mull

Dun I (pronounced Doon Ee) is the highest point of Iona, and this short walk is for those who simply want to get an aerial view of the north part of the island. There are two other walks on the island of greater length, and this brief ascent of Dun I can be combined with Walk 4.7 easily enough. Despite its modest height, Dun I does offer a lovely viewpoint, especially in a north-easterly direction to Ardmeanach and more to the north to Ulva and the Treshnish headland beyond. Due north are the scattered Treshnish Isles, among which the shapely Dutchman's Cap is easily picked out. In fact, as Dun I is visible from most parts of the island, it follows that it proves a good vantage point from which to study the hummocks and hollows.

On leaving the ferry, take the first turning on the right, passing the **post office** and walking in front of a row of cottages, guests houses and a small hotel. At the end of the row, a path leads up to join the main island road. Here, turn right, and continue past the **abbey**, walking on to pass a **memorial cross**, just beyond which, at **Auchabhaich**, at a gate and signpost on the left you can leave the road and cross a field to the foot of Dun I.

A comfortable path climbs to the left and then moves back, climbing more steeply, and soon bringing the large shapely cairn on top of **Dun I** into view. A cylindrical trig pillar stands nearby, and from it there is fine view northwards to the top end of the island, the sands of Traigh an t-Suidhe and the little island of Eilean Annraidh.

The naturalist and writer **Thomas Pennant** came this way in 1772, and instructs that 'the traveller must not neglect to ascend the hill of Dun-ii; from whose summit is a most picturesque view of the long chain of little islands, neighbours to this; of the long low isles of Col and Tir-I to the west; and the vast height of Rum and Skie to the north.' It is sound advice.

Retrace your steps to the **ferry slip**.

Dun I

189

WALK 4.7

A northerly circuit

Start/Finish	Iona ferry slip (NM286240)
Distance	9.5km (6 miles)
Total ascent	200m (655ft)
Terrain	Road walking; coastal machair and rocky outcrops
Map	OS Explorer 373 Iona, Staffa and Ross of Mull

A fine walk to the northern end of the island, and from there round the north-west coastline to reach the idyllic beach, Camas Cùil an t-Saimh. Once beyond the northernmost point, the walking becomes a little more challenging at times, but there is a continuous path throughout, although there is a measure of enjoyment in exploring as you potter along. What is important, however, is, as elsewhere on Mull and Iona, to recognise that the land you cross is working farmland: keep dogs under control, and, for those who like to camp wild, do not assume that you can do so indiscriminately. Seek permission first.

From the ferry walk forward to the second turning on the right, passing (and ideally exploring briefly) the 12th-century **nunnery**. Turn right after this (or if you visited the nunnery exit its grounds) onto the main road to the northern end of the island. Keep on past the **abbey**, and, later, past the turning up to Dun I, although this (Walk 4.6) could easily be added to the walk.

Press on beyond the end of the lane and up to the northern tip of the island. To the east, Traigh Bhàn, and to the west, Traigh an t-Suidhe, are both fine sandy beaches, and will prove satisfactory endpoints for many visitors. But otherwise, turn west, following the course of Traigh an t-Suidhe, and then the north-west coastline, moving among and over or round low hillocks and mini-glens as

you go, and eventually saunter down to the machair rafts inland from the lovely **Camas Cuil an t-Saimh**.

The northern tip of Iona

Here, turn inland, following a broad track across the **golf course** you find there, and soon leaving the common grazings when you reach the end of a cross-island surfaced lane. Follow this lane to NM278236, where rough tracks appear right and left. Turn left here, and follow the track for about 300m (984ft), until you can swing right and follow an on-going track back to the **ferry**. Or you can simply stay on the surfaced lane, and this will take you to the same place.

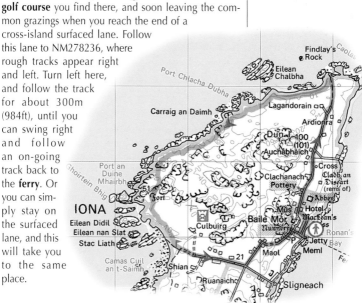

WALK 4.8

Port na Curaich

Start/Finish	Iona ferry slip
Distance	8km (5 miles)
Total ascent	165m (540ft)
Terrain	Rugged moorland; some road walking
Map	OS Explorer 373 Iona, Staffa and Ross of Mull

Port na Curaich lies at the southern end of Iona, and the name translates as 'the port or harbour of the coracle', this being the spot where Columba is thought to have landed in AD563 on his journey from Ireland. There is a path across the island to the south end leading to Port an Fhir-bhrèige and Port na Curaich, the two bays separated by a low headland. From here a moorland path, probably a quarryman's track, offers a less orthodox way back to the ferry.

As you step off the ferry, take the first road on the left, past the café-bar, and walk along the narrow road, at first parallel with the shore and then changing direction to strike across the heart of the island to the common grazings on the far side. Here you find a **golf course**, and how inconsequential its challenges, albeit mainly ovine deposits, must be on a day of warm sun and gentle breezes.

Ahead, across the springy machair, the white sands of **Camas Cùil an t-Saimh** await, a glorious sight, a great sandy arc punctuated by rocky islets and wannabe islands.

Machair is the Scottish name for the short, springy turf found along the Atlantic coasts of Scotland; it is a delight to walk on. It also makes a passable golf course – possibly not championship standard but the original nine-hole course of Iona was developed as long ago as 1895, and extended 10 years later to a full 18 holes.

Camas Cùil an t-Saimh

Many visitors walk just this far, sit among the low dunes, contemplate the wonders of Nature, and forget the time of day. If landscapes, or in this case seascapes, can be mesmeric, then this is; one of the most soothing, comforting, gratifying nooks to be found anywhere.

ST COLUMBA AND THE END OF DAYS

Perhaps it is the association of this spot and this island with the man who was to become St Columba, that gives rise to the claim that 'Seven years before the end of the world, a deluge shall drown the nations: the sea, at one tide, shall cover Ireland, and the green-headed Ilay (Islay), but Columba's isle shall swim above the flood'; all of which sounds like a good reason for stocking up on Islay malt whiskies, and possibly explains why there are so many crowned heads, from different nations, and one Labour politician, interred on Iona.

It is a popular misconception that Columba came to Iona to import Christianity. As a plan, this was not true; as a consequence, it was.

Columba was an Irish prince, and credited with the first breach of copyright. The problem arose when a monk returned from Rome with a copy of the first Vulgate Gospels to be seen in Ireland. So impressed was he with the text that Columba made a copy of the gospels without first seeking consent – hence breach of copyright. He was ordered to give up his copy by the High King of Ireland, who pronounced, 'To every cow its calf, and to every book its copy.' Columba refused the order and so instigated the Battle of Cul Dremne in AD561. Columba's followers prevailed, but he was so overcome by the grief that his stubbornness had wrought and the blood it had spilled, that he determined to leave Ireland, never to return, and imposed the condition that he would not settle anywhere within sight of Ireland. And so it was that with 12 companions of unrecorded enthusiasm he set sail in a coracle – a framework of wood covered with tarred hides – landing first on the Garvelloch Islands in the Firth of Lorn. But from there Columba could still see Ireland, and so moved on, this time to land on Iona, at Port na Curaich. It was here on Iona that he founded his abbey from which he would set out to convert the pagan tribes of Scotland.

Turn left (south) parallel with the coast, walking along the edge of the golf course. In the distance, along the rocky coast, the Spouting Cave often puts on a splendid

Loch Staoineig

display, sending plumes of sea spray high into the air. Then take to a grassy vehicle track that strikes obliquely across the course to a distant building, beyond which you see a fence. Walk on, and up, beside the fence, leaving the golf course behind, and climbing into a rocky, moorland terrain and heather and bracken.

Loch Staoineig is a surprise, and, set against a seaward ripple of islands, suddenly pops into view following a gentle climb. From here, the path rounds the loch to begin a gradual descent to **Port an Fhir-bhrèige** and **Port na Curaich** where a huge swathe of sea-washed pebbles are met.

These **pebbles** were, allegedly, piled high by monks as penance for their sins. Thomas Pennant, who visited Iona in 1772, referred to 'a small bay, with a pebbly beach, mixed with variety of pretty stones…a vast tract…covered with heaps of stones, of unequal sizes: these…were the penances of monks who were to raise heaps of dimensions equal to their crimes: and to judge by some, it is no breach of charity to think there were among them enormous sinners.'

There are two ways back to the ferry, one more ambitious than the other. The easiest is to retrace your steps, not in any way a hardship, and offering the advantage of another bout of inner contemplation at the sands of Camas Cùil an t-Saimh. The other crosses the more rugged, but no less agreeable, landscape of the south-east of the island. There is a continuous grassy path all the way; it is just a question of locating the start.

Backtrack towards the grassy sward where you first came down to the bays, and look for a narrow path climbing easily through the low rocks of **An t-Aird**. After an uncertain start, the path soon becomes obvious as it twists and turns around outcrops, and offers tempting variations (all of which can be used to explore this lovely headland), but after a short period heading eastwards, the trend becomes more north-easterly as you cross the moorland, which, although wet in a few places, is only making a token gesture in that direction.

Eventually, the path leads down to a metal gate at NM276232 giving into a wide, enclosed track that leads out past the cottage at **Rùanaich** to the cross-island road used earlier in the walk. On reaching the road, turn right, and retrace your steps to the **ferry**.

WALK 4.9

Erraid

Start/Finish	Knockvologan (NM314204); limited parking
Distance	Variable – 5.5km (3½ miles) minimum
Total ascent	Variable – 140m (460ft) minimum
Terrain	Rough farm pasture; tidal sand flats; undulating heather and rock moorland
Map	OS Explorer 373 Iona, Staffa and Ross of Mull

Erraid is a tidal island at the extreme western edge of the Ross of Mull, south of Fionnphort, accessible for a few hours either side of low tide by a simple walk across a white-sand strand. The island itself is all hummocks and hollows, and a delight to explore. There are no paths to speak of, save those made by sheep.

Drive to the remote farmsteads at Knockvologan. If you continue to the very end of the surfaced road, it may be possible to park one or two cars out of the way of farm equipment. Failing that, back along the road the same applies at the farm buildings near the start of Walk 3.6, at the turning for Tireragan. There is also limited roadside parking in a number of places. At all times, please park considerately; this is an active farming community.

At the road end, take to a descending track that curves downwards, and soon reaches the tidal inlet of **Bàgh a' Chnoic Mhaoileanaich**. Bear a little to the right towards a metal gate, but then keep to the left of a fence and walk round to a suitable crossing point.

From here, the choice of route is entirely yours. You can cross directly to **Erraid**, or turn northwards, walking along the white sands to step onto the island at its north-eastern end.

Wherever you reach the island, you can wander freely. The landscape is one of numerous granite upthrusts, decked with heather and birch, interspersed with wetter ground, most of which can be evaded.

With good timing, and an understanding of the tide tables (available at a number of shops and tourist information centres), you can spend a few enjoyable hours on the island, before heading back across to 'mainland' Mull.

ERRAID

Erraid was a lighthouse shore station until 1967, and an observatory on the highest point, Crioc Mor (NM296202), was used for signalling to the lighthouses. At the southern end of the island, Tràigh Gheal is also known as Balfour Bay, being the place were David Balfour, principal character in Robert Louis Stevenson's novel Kidnapped, made landfall after he was shipwrecked on the Torran Rocks, and where he spent four miserable days without shelter, living off shellfish, before he realised that the island was tidal.

Stevenson, of course, was one of the renowned family of lighthouse builders, and as a young man he spent time on Erraid during the building of the Dhu Heartach Lighthouse, which marks a treacherous rock 24km (15 miles) out to the south-west in the Firth of Lorn. The lighthouse was deemed necessary to fill the dark gap between the Skerryvore and Rhinns of Islay lights. Building material for the lighthouse was quarried on Erraid, and ferried over to Dhu Heartach when the workmen – who lived in a temporary cage over the reef – signalled that it was safe to land. The first tier of stones was laid in 1869, and the work completed two years later; the lighthouse was 'turned on' in 1872.

Striding out for Erraid

APPENDIX 1
Essential and supplementary reading

Boswell, James. *The Journal of a Tour to the Hebrides with Samuel Johnson LLD* (London: J M Dent: Everyman, Ernest Rhys, ed, 1909)

Brooks, J A. *Mull, Iona and Staffa* (Norwich: Jarrold Publishing, 1983–1993)

Craig, David. *On the Crofters' Trail* (London: Jonathan Cape, 1990)

Crumley, Jim.
— *The Heart of Mull* (Colin Baxter Photography, 1996)
— *Among Islands* (Mainstream Publishing, 1994)

Currie, Jo. *Mull: The Island and its People* (Edinburgh: Birlinn, 2001)

Haldane, A R B. *The Drove Roads of Scotland* (Colonsay: House of Lochar, 1995)

Haswell-Smith, Hamish. *The Scottish Islands* (Edinburgh: Canongate, 1996, 2004, 2008)

Hedderwick, Mairi. *An Eye on the Hebrides: An Illustrated Journey* (Edinburgh: Canongate Publishing, 1989)

Johnson, Samuel. *A Journey to the Western Islands of Scotland* (Penguin Books, 1993)

Jones, Rosalind. *Mull in the making* (Self-published: Craigmore, Mull, 1997)

LeMay, Jackie. *Glen More: A drive through history* (Tobermory: Brown and Whittaker, 2001)

MacArthur, E Mairi. *Columba's Island: Iona from Past to Present* (Edinburgh: Edinburgh University Press, 1995)

MacDonald, Hugh. *Guide to Staffa, Iona and Mull* (Oban: self-published, nd)

MacKenzie, Ann. *Island voices: Traditions of North Mull* (Edinburgh: Birlinn, 2002)

Macnab, Peter.
— *Mull and Iona* (Newton Abbot: David and Charles/Pevensey, 1995–2008)
— *Mull and Iona: Highways and Byways* (Edinburgh: Luath Press, 1986–2003)

Marsh, Terry. *The Magic of the Scottish Islands* (Newton Abbot: David and Charles, 2002 and 2008 pbk), illustrated by Jon Sparks

Morton, H V. *In Search of Scotland* (London: Methuen & Co, 1929)

Orr, Willie. *Discovering Argyll, Mull and Iona* (Edinburgh: John Donald, 1990)

Pennant, Thomas. *A Tour in Scotland and Voyage to the Hebrides, 1772* (Chester: John Monk, 1774 and 1776; Edinburgh: Birlinn Ltd., 1998)

Prebble, John. *The Highland Clearances* (London: Secker and Warburg, 1963, Penguin Books, 1969–1977)

Scott, Sir Walter.
— *The Lord of the Isles* (Edinburgh: Adam and Charles Black, 1857)
— *Northern Lights: A Voyage in the Lighthouse Yacht to Nova Zembla and the Lord knows where in the Summer of 1814* (Byways Books, William F Laughlan, ed, 1982)

Semple, John Mackenzie. *The Stones of Iona: The Black Monks and the Lords of the Isles* (Glasgow: Iona Community Publishing Department, 1964 and 1967)

Stevenson, Robert Louis. *Kidnapped: being Memoirs of the Adventures of David Balfour in the year 1751* (London: James Henderson; Edinburgh: Canongate, 2006)

Swire, Otta F. *The Inner Hebrides and their Legends* (London: Collins, 1964)

Tranter, Nigel. *The Story of Scotland* (Moffat: Lochar Publishing, 1991)

De Watteville, Alastair. *The Isle of Mull* (Romsey: Romsey Fine Art, 1994)

Whittaker, Jean. *Mull: Monuments and History* (Tobermory: Brown and Whittaker, 2004)

Wilson, Eunice. *Night on Ben Talaidh* (Tobermory: Brown and Whittaker, 2005)

APPENDIX 2
Glossary of Gaelic words

Gaelic	English	Gaelic	English
aber	mouth or confluence of a river	cala(dh)	harbour
abhainn	river	camas	channel or creek
acarseid	anchorage	caol	kyle, strait, narrow
achadh	field or park	carn	cairn, pile of stones
ailean	green field	cioch	woman's breast
a(i)rd	high promontory	clach	stone
airidh	shieling	clachan	village
allt	burn	cladagh	shore or beach
aros	house	cladh	churchyard
ath	ford	clais	hollow
bac	bank	cleit	ridge
b(h)a(i)gh	bay	cnap	hillock
b(h)aile	town	cnoc, cnok, knock	small hill
b(h)an	white		
barr	top or summit	coille	wood or forest
b(h)e(a)g	little	coire	corrie
bealach	pass or col	creag	crag or cliff
bearn	gap	cro	sheep pen
beinne	ben or hill	cruach	stack or heap
beithe	birch tree	darach	oak wood
bo	cow (plural ba)	dearg	red
bodach	old man	druim	ridge
bog	soft or damp	dubh	black or dark
brae	top or summit	dun	mound or fort
b(h)reac	speckled	each	horse
brua(i)ch	steep hillside	ear	east
b(h)uidhe	yellow	eas	waterfall
burn	stream	eilach	watercourse
cailleach	old woman	eilean	island
caisteal	castle	fada	long

Gaelic	English	Gaelic	English
faich	meadow	mol	shingly beach
fank	sheep pen	monadh	moor, hill
faoghail	ford, sea channel	moine	mossy
fasgadh	shelter	m(h)or	large, tall
fraoch	heather	mullach	summit
fuar	cold	ob	bay, creek
fuaran	spring or well	odhar	dappled
garbh	rough or harsh	or	gold
geal	bright	ord	conical hill
geo, geodha	narrow cove	os	outlet of lake or river
gil	narrow glen	poll, puill	pond
glais	stream	ruadh	red, reddish
glas	grey or green	rubha, rudha	headland
gleann	glen or valley	sean	old
gob	point or beak	sgarbh	cormorant
gobhar	goat	sga(i)t	skate
inbhir	rivermouth, bay	sgeir	skerry
iolaire	eagle	sgurr, sgorr	peak
lagan	hollow	sith	fairy
lairig	pass or sloping face of a hill	sithean	fairy hill
leac	flat stone	slochd	deep hollow
learg	hillside	srath	valley
leathad	slope or declevity	sron	promontory
leathan	broad	stac	stack
leitir	slope	stob	point
liath	grey	strath	river valley
linne	sound or channel	stuc	pinnacle, peak
loch	lake	suidhe	resting place
lon	stream marsh	traigh	beach
machair	low grassy land	t(a)igh	house
mam	gently rising hill	tulach	hillock
maol	headland	uaimh	cave
meadhon	middle	uig	bay
meall	rounded hill	uisge	water, rain
mointeach	moorland		

APPENDIX 3
Useful information and contact details

Tourist Information Offices
Pick up a free copy of the Travel Guide for the isles of Mull and Iona, published twice yearly. The guide contains all essential travel information for getting about the islands, including current bus and ferry timetables. Also worth picking up are the monthly Round and About Mull & Iona (price 50p; www.roundandaboutmull.co.uk), and Mull and Iona Life (price 55p). As well as editorial and advertorial, they contain current information about what's happening on the islands, including roadworks and closures, special events, markets and the like.

For a comprehensive directory of facilities and services on the islands you need *The Red Book* for Mull and Iona (telephone directory) (price £6, available from post offices and stores).

Craignure (all year)
Tel: 01680 812377 or 01680 812556;
email: mull@visitscotland.com

Tobermory (seasonal)
Tel: 01688 302182;
email: tobermory@visitscotland.com

Banks

Clydesdale Bank, Tobermory
Tel: 08457 240024

There are cash machines at numerous outlets across the island, including most supermarkets.

Camping and Caravan Sites
Balmeanach Park, Fishnish
Tel: 01680 300342
Fidden Farm, Fionnphort
Tel: 01681 700213
Killiechronan Campsite, Loch na Keal
Tel: 07747 192443
Tobermory Campsite, Dervaig Road
Tel: 01688 302624

Iona
Cnoc Oran
Tel: 01681 700112

Chemists
Tobermory Pharmacy, 46 Main Street
Tel: 01688 302431
Also in Spar grocers, Bunessan

Doctors
Bunessan Tel: 01681 700261
Salen Tel: 01680 300327
Tobermory Tel: 01688 302013

Dentist
Tobermory Tel: 01688 302105

Garages/Petrol Pumps
Bayview Garage, Craignure
Tel: 01680 812444;
Mobile: 07774 256267
Black's Garage, Salen
Tel: 01680 300364
Craignure Stores, Craignure
Tel: 01680 812301
Kennedy's Garage, Salen
Tel: 01680 300396
R MacCallum, Ardfenaig, Bunessan
Tel: 01681 700206

McDowell's Garage, Killiechronan
Tel: 01680 300666
Mackay's Garage, Tobermory
Tel: 01688 302103
Rowley's Filling Station, Salen
Tel: 01680 300326

Hospital
Dunaros Hospital, Salen
Tel: 01680 300392

Mountain Rescue
Dial 999.

Police
In an emergency, dial 999, otherwise
you can contact the police on the
following numbers.
Bunessan Tel: 01681 700222
Craignure Tel: 01680 812322
Salen Tel: 01680 300322
Tobermory Tel: 01688 302016

Post Offices
Aros and Salen Tel: 01680 300321
Bunessan Tel: 01681 700252
Craignure Tel: 01680 812301
Dervaig Tel: 01688 400208
Fionnphort Tel: 01681 700470
Iona Tel: 01681 700515
Lochbuie Tel: 01680 814225
Lochdon Tel: 01680 812391
Pennyghael Tel: 01681 704229
Tobermory Tel: 01688 302058
Ulva Ferry Tel: 01688 500245

Public Transport
Because of seasonal variations it is
essential to obtain timetables from the
Tourist Information Offices.

Bowmans Coaches
Scallastle, Craignure, Isle of Mull
Tel: 01680 812313
Service 494: Tobermory – Dervaig
  – Calgary

Service 495: Craignure – Salen
  – Tobermory
Service 496: Craignure – Bunessan
  – Fionnphort

Morrison Bus Service
Tel: 01688 302220
Tobermory – Calgary

Supermarkets
Spar (Bunessan, Craignure, Iona,
Tobermory and Salen)
Co-op (Tobermory)

Vets
Fishnish Tel: 01680 300319

Youth Hostels
Not all hostels are open all year; please
contact them for details.

Independent Hostels
Iona Hostel, Iona, Argyll PA76 6SW
Tel: 01681 700781
Dervaig Bunkrooms, Dervaig Village
Hall, Dervaig, Isle of Mull, Argyll
PA75 6QN
Tel: 01688 400491;
www.bunkrooms.mull-scotland.co.uk

Glenaros Lodge, Aros, Salen,
Isle of Mull, Argyll PA72 6JP
Tel: 01680 300301;
www.glenaroslodge.net

Scottish Youth Hostels Association
7 Glebe Crescent, Stirling FK8 2JA
Tel: 01786 891400;
Fax: 01786 891333;
Central bookings: 0870 1 55 32 55;
reservations@syha.org.uk;
www.syha.org.uk

Tobermory Youth Hostel
Tel: 01688 302481

Mull and Iona Estates

Note: Only landholdings over 1000 acres are shown.

1	Glengorm	01688 302321
2	Ardnacross	01680 300371
3	Antuim	01688 400230
4	Glen Aros	01631 770369
5	Tenga	01688 400230
6	Calgary	01688 400248
7	Treshnish	01688 400249
8	Torloisk	01688 400341
9	Killiechronan	01680 300403
10	Oskamull	01688 500245
11	Ulva	01688 500264
12	Gometra	01688 500221
13	Benmore	01680 300229
14	Gruline	01680 300332
15	Glen Forsa	01680 300674
16	Torosay	01680 812421
17	Auchnacraig	0131 226 7744
18	Ardura	01680 812199
19	Kinlochspelve	01680 814214
20	Croggan	01680 814214
21	Laggan	01680 814214
22	Ben Buie	01680 814214
23	Glenbyre	01680 814214
24	Rossal	01681 704252
25	Ardvergnish	01681 704252
26	Kilfinichen, Balnahard and Ballymeanach	01681 705229
27a	Burg	01681 705229
27b	Iona	08444 932242
28	Carsaig	01681 704202
29	Pennyghael	01681 704232
30	Ormsaig	01681 704032
31	Scoor and Beach	01681 700087
32	Scoor Estate	01681 700087
33	Argyll Estates	01681 700307
34	Ardalanish	01681 700265
35	Erraid and Knockvologan	01681 700372

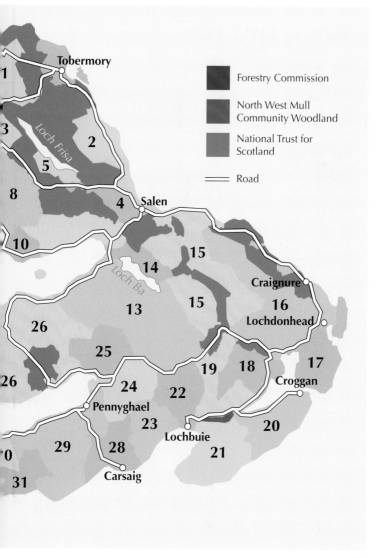

INDEX

CICERONE GUIDES TO THE BRITISH ISLES

**BRITISH ISLES CHALLENGES,
COLLECTIONS AND ACTIVITIES**
The End to End Trail
The Mountains of England and Wales
  1 Wales
  2 England
The National Trails
The Relative Hills of Britain
The Ridges of England, Wales and
  Ireland
The UK Trailwalker's Handbook
Three Peaks, Ten Tors
MOUNTAIN LITERATURE
Unjustifiable Risk?
UK CYCLING
Border Country Cycle Routes
Cycling in the Peak District
Lands End to John O'Groats Cycle
  Guide
Mountain Biking in the Lake District
The Lancashire Cycleway
SCOTLAND
Backpacker's Britain
  Central and Southern Scottish
  Highlands
  Northern Scotland
Ben Nevis and Glen Coe
North to the Cape
Not the West Highland Way
Scotland's Best Small Mountains
Scotland's Far West
Scotland's Mountain Ridges
Scrambles in Lochaber
The Border Country
The Central Highlands
The Great Glen Way
The Isle of Mull
The Isle of Skye
The Pentland Hills: A Walker's Guide
The Southern Upland Way
The Speyside Way
The West Highland Way
Walking in Scotland's Far North
Walking in the Cairngorms
Walking in the Hebrides
Walking in the Ochils, Campsie Fells
  and Lomond Hills
Walking in Torridon
Walking Loch Lomond and the
  Trossachs
Walking on Harris and Lewis
Walking on Jura, Islay and Colonsay
Walking on the Isle of Arran
Walking on the Orkney and Shetland
  Isles
Walking the Galloway Hills
Walking the Lowther Hills
Walking the Munros
  1 Southern, Central and Western
  Highlands
  2 Northern Highlands and the
  Cairngorms

Winter Climbs Ben Nevis and
  Glen Coe
Winter Climbs in the Cairngorms
World Mountain Ranges: Scotland
NORTHERN ENGLAND TRAILS
A Northern Coast to Coast Walk
Backpacker's Britain
  Northern England
Hadrian's Wall Path
The Dales Way
The Pennine Way
The Spirit of Hadrian's Wall
**NORTH EAST ENGLAND,
YORKSHIRE DALES AND PENNINES**
Historic Walks in North Yorkshire
South Pennine Walks
The Cleveland Way and the
  Yorkshire Wolds Way
The North York Moors
The Reivers Way
The Teesdale Way
The Yorkshire Dales Angler's Guide
The Yorkshire Dales
  North and East
  South and West
Walking in County Durham
Walking in Northumberland
Walking in the North Pennines
Walking in the Wolds
Walks in Dales Country
Walks in the Yorkshire Dales
Walks on the North York Moors
  Books 1 & 2
**NORTH WEST ENGLAND AND THE
ISLE OF MAN**
A Walker's Guide to the Lancaster
  Canal
Historic Walks in Cheshire
Isle of Man Coastal Path
The Isle of Man
The Ribble Way
Walking in Lancashire
Walking in the Forest of Bowland
  and Pendle
Walking on the West Pennine Moors
Walks in Lancashire Witch Country
Walks in Ribble Country
Walks in Silverdale and Arnside
Walks in the Forest of Bowland
LAKE DISTRICT
Coniston Copper Mines
Great Mountain Days in the Lake
  District
Lake District Winter Climbs
Lakeland Fellranger
  The Central Fells
  The Mid-Western Fells
  The Near Eastern Fells
  The Southern Fells
Roads and Tracks of the Lake District
Rocky Rambler's Wild Walks

Scrambles in the Lake District
  North & South
Short Walks in Lakeland
  1 South Lakeland
  2 North Lakeland
  3 West Lakeland
The Cumbria Coastal Way
The Cumbria Way and the Allerdale
  Ramble
The Lake District Anglers' Guide
Tour of the Lake District
**DERBYSHIRE, PEAK DISTRICT AND
MIDLANDS**
High Peak Walks
The Star Family Walks
Walking in Derbyshire
White Peak Walks
  The Northern Dales
  The Southern Dales
SOUTHERN ENGLAND
A Walker's Guide to the Isle of
  Wight
London – The definitive walk-
  ing guide
The Cotswold Way
The Greater Ridgeway
The Lea Valley Walk
The North Downs Way
The South Downs Way
The South West Coast Path
The Thames Path
Walking in Bedfordshire
Walking in Berkshire
Walking in Buckinghamshire
Walking in Kent
Walking in Sussex
Walking in the Isles of Scilly
Walking in the Thames Valley
Walking on Dartmoor
WALES AND WELSH BORDERS
Backpacker's Britain
  Wales
Glyndwr's Way
Great Mountain Days in Snowdonia
Hillwalking in Snowdonia
Hillwalking in Wales
  Vols 1 & 2
Offa's Dyke Path
Ridges of Snowdonia
Scrambles in Snowdonia
The Ascent of Snowdon
The Lleyn Peninsula Coastal Path
The Pembrokeshire Coastal Path
The Shropshire Hills
The Spirit Paths of Wales
Walking in Pembrokeshire
Walking on the Brecon Beacons
Welsh Winter Climbs

For full information on all our British
and international guides, please visit
our website: **www.cicerone.co.uk**.

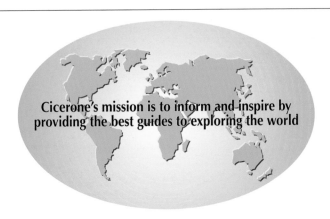

Cicerone's mission is to inform and inspire by providing the best guides to exploring the world

Since its foundation 40 years ago, Cicerone has specialised in publishing guidebooks and has built a reputation for quality and reliability. It now publishes nearly 300 guides to the major destinations for outdoor enthusiasts, including Europe, UK and the rest of the world.

Written by leading and committed specialists, Cicerone guides are recognised as the most authoritative. They are full of information, maps and illustrations so that the user can plan and complete a successful and safe trip or expedition – be it a long face climb, a walk over Lakeland fells, an alpine cycling tour, a Himalayan trek or a ramble in the countryside.

With a thorough introduction to assist planning, clear diagrams, maps and colour photographs to illustrate the terrain and route, and accurate and detailed text, Cicerone guides are designed for ease of use and access to the information.

If the facts on the ground change, or there is any aspect of a guide that you think we can improve, we are always delighted to hear from you.

Cicerone Press
2 Police Square Milnthorpe Cumbria LA7 7PY
Tel: 015395 62069 Fax: 015395 63417
info@cicerone.co.uk www.cicerone.co.uk